TSUI HARK'S
Zu: Warriors From the Magic Mountain

T0351394

Hong Kong University Press thanks Xu Bing for writing the Press's name in his Square Word Calligraphy for the covers of its books. For further information see p. iv.

THE NEW HONG KONG CINEMA SERIES

Series General Editors

Ackbar Abbas
Wimal Dissanayake

Series Advisors

Chris Berry
Nick Browne
Ann Hui
Leo Lee
Li Cheuk-to
Patricia Mellencamp
Meaghan Morris
Paul Willemen
Peter Wollen
Wu Hung

✦ ✦ ✦ ✦ ✦

Other titles in the series

John Woo's *A Better Tomorrow*
Karen Fang

Wong Kar-wai's *Ashes of Time*
Wimal Dissanayake

Wong Kar-wai's *Happy Together*
Jeremy Tambling

TSUI HARK'S
Zu: Warriors From the Magic Mountain

Andrew Schroeder

香港大學出版社
HONG KONG UNIVERSITY PRESS

Hong Kong University Press
14/F Hing Wai Centre
7 Tin Wan Praya Road
Aberdeen
Hong Kong

www.hkupress.org
(secure on-line ordering)

British Library Cataloguing-in-Publication Data
A catalogue record for this book is available from the British Library.

Printed and bound by Caritas Printing Training Centre, Hong Kong, China

Hong Kong University Press is honoured that Xu Bing, whose
art explores the complex themes of language across cultures,
has written the Press's name in his Square Word Calligraphy.
This signals our commitment to cross-cultural thinking and the
distinctive nature of our English-language books published in
China.

"At first glance, Square Word Calligraphy appears to be nothing
more unusual than Chinese characters, but in fact it is a new
way of rendering English words in the format of a square so they
resemble Chinese characters. Chinese viewers expect to be able
to read Square Word Calligraphy but cannot. Western viewers,
however are surprised to find they can read it. Delight erupts
when meaning is unexpectedly revealed."
— Britta Erickson, *The Art of Xu Bing*

Contents

Series Preface

The New Hong Kong cinema came into existence under very special circumstances, during a period of social and political crisis resulting in a change of cultural paradigms. Such critical moments have produced the cinematic achievements of the early Soviet cinema, neorealism, the "nouvelle vague," the German cinema in the 70s and, we can now say, the recent Hong Kong cinema. If this cinema grew increasingly intriguing in the 1980s, after the announcement of Hong Kong's return to China, it was largely because it had to confront a new cultural and political space that was both complex and hard to define, where the problems of colonialism were overlaid with those of globalism in an uncanny way. Such uncanniness could not be caught through straight documentary or conventional history writing; it was left to the cinema to define it.

It does so by presenting to us an urban space that slips away if we try to grasp it too directly, a space that cinema coaxes into existence by whatever means at its disposal. Thus it is by eschewing a narrow idea of relevance and pursuing disreputable genres like melodrama, kung fu and the fantastic that cinema brings into view something else about the city which could otherwise be missed. One classic example is Stanley Kwan's *Rouge*, which draws on the unrealistic form of the ghost story to evoke something of the uncanniness of Hong Kong's urban space. It takes a ghost to catch a ghost.

In the new Hong Kong cinema, then, it is neither the subject matter nor a particular generic conventions that is paramount. In fact, many Hong Kong films begin by following generic conventions but proceed to transform them. Such transformation of genre is also the transformation of a sense of place where all the rules have quietly and deceptively changed. It is this shifting sense of place, often expressed negatively and indirectly — but in the best work always rendered precisely in (necessarily) innovative images — that is decisive for the New Hong Kong Cinema.

Has the creative period of the New Hong Kong Cinema come to an end? However we answer the question, here is a need now to evaluate the achievements of Hong Kong cinema. During the last few years, a number of full-length books have appeared, testifying to the topicality of the subject. These books survey the field with varying degrees of success, but there is yet an almost complete lack of authoritative texts focusing in depth on individual Hong Kong films. This book series on the New Hong Kong Cinema is designed to fill this lack. Each volume will be written by a scholar/critic who will analyse each chosen film in detail and provide a critical apparatus for further discussion including filmography and bibliography.

Our objective is to produce a set of interactional and provocative readings that would make a self-aware intervention into modern Hong Kong culture. We advocate no one theoretical position; the authors will approach their chosen films from their own distinct points of vantage and interest. The aim of the series is to generate open-ended discussions of the selected films, employing diverse analytical strategies, in order to urge the readers towards self-reflective engagements with the films in particular and the Hong Kong cultural space in general. It is our hope that this series will contribute to the sharpening of Hong Kong culture's conceptions of itself.

In keeping with our conviction that film is not a self-enclosed signification system but an important cultural practice among similar others, we wish to explore how films both reflect and inflect culture. And it is useful to keep in mind that reflection of reality and realty of reflection are equally important in the understanding of cinema.

Ackbar Abbas
Wimal Dissanayake

Series General Editors

Acknowledgments

This book, like all books, was only possible to write with the aid of a great number of people. First and foremost, I am deeply grateful to Christine Choy for taking the chance to allow me to teach for two unforgettable semesters at the City University of Hong Kong's School of Creative Media. Her example of intellectual risk and creative experimentation continues to inspire me, and my ideas for this book would never have formed without the experience she helped to provide. In a similar sense, this book is dedicated in part to everyone I worked with at SCM during that time, many of whom helped me more than they know through their conversations and their friendship. In particular I'd like to thank Philip Lee, Theresa Mikuria, Steve Fore and Nancy Tong. As always, my dissertation advisor at NYU, Thomas Bender, deserves my endless gratitude for his broadmindedness, his patience and for helping to teach me what it means to be a responsible citizen of the world. The same goes for Andrew Ross, Nikhil Pal Singh, Toby Miller, Lisa Duggan, Phillip Brian Harper and Todd Gitlin, all of whom have helped to make the NYU American Studies Program a model for the radical transformation not only of American Studies but of America itself. Thanks is also due to my current friends and colleagues at the University of Wisconsin – Oshkosh, especially Ralph Beliveau, Sarah Nilsen, Tony Palmeri and Flora Stapel, for providing a stimulating and secure intellectual environment in the wilds of the Midwestern US. At a slightly more distant remove, I have always wanted to have the opportunity to thank my good friend and former advisor James Livingston, who I hold primarily responsible for teaching me to think unusual thoughts at an early age. And it goes without saying, of course, that I am very grateful to everyone involved in the book, particularly the Series Editors Ackbar Abbas and Wimal Dissanayake, and Mina Kumar and Delphine Ip at the Hong Kong University Press, for tracking me down after the Center for Asian Studies conference in December 2001, and for guiding me through the strange process of writing and publishing my first book.

Last, but never least, my undying love and my eternal thanks goes to my wife, Jennifer.

1

Seeing Past the Future:
An Introduction to *Zu:*
Warriors From the Magic Mountain

Among the many great films of the Hong Kong New Wave, few
were more unusual in concept, scope, or eventual patterns of
influence than Tsui Hark's *Zu: Warriors From the Magic
Mountain*. Released in 1983, it was quickly dubbed Hong Kong's
version of *Star Wars*. The comparison was both a form of praise
and of blame, of hope and of resignation, of modernization and
capitulation. As such, many critics rightly interpreted *Zu: Warriors
From the Magic Mountain* as a key document of Hong Kong's
conflicted construction of a new social identity in between
colonialism and globalism during its post-colonial and post-
industrial transitions.

Despite the film's backward-looking mythology, *Zu: Warriors
From the Magic Mountain* pitched itself as a forward-looking
intervention into the debates over the politics of Hong Kong's
transitional identity. As the critic Lisa Morton writes, "*Zu* is
sometimes referred to as the Chinese *Star Wars*, but where George
Lucas' space fantasy reaffirms existing values ... *Zu* is a far more

complex social document."[1] In the most congratulatory interpretations of the film's contribution to Hong Kong's contemporary cultural scene, *Zu* was a pop-political allegory par excellence. It signified the remarkable capacity of Hong Kong cinema to employ big-screen commercial spectacle, including such lowbrow fare as Hollywood special effects technologies and comic-book storytelling, for the sake of complex and sophisticated social ideas.

At the same time, many interpretations of *Zu: Warriors*, especially those situating the film within the context of Tsui Hark's career as a whole, have downplayed it as an example of what David Bordwell calls the "lost promise" of the Hong Kong New Wave. For some, the more invidious comparisons to *Star Wars*, or of Tsui himself to Steven Spielberg, persist even in the face of *Zu*'s manifest economic failure and its general inability to spark a similarly rapid and immediate technological mutation in Hong Kong cinema to what Lucas and Spielberg achieved in Hollywood. Strangely, many current reviewers tend to assume without proof that *Zu: Warriors* must have been a financial success given its close cultural association with films of such gargantuan financial proportions and questionable narrative depth. According to Bordwell, this kind of interpretation argues that, "Tsui lost interest in social provocation and channeled his energies into noisy lowbrow entertainment. He recycled old movies and tired genres while shamelessly copying Hollywood trends."[2] In those terms, *Zu*'s overtures to globally popular cultural trends took Hong Kong cinema further and further away from the serious social and cultural possibilities of the New Wave while making Hong Kong cinema safe in the long run for the full-frontal incursion of global Hollywood.

Neither of these interpretations is entirely true, nor entirely wrong, yet each is equally incomplete. One way to frame the broad aim of this book is to say that it carves a path between them in order to re-describe *Zu: Warriors From the Magic Mountain* as a key moment in much larger historical trends. *Zu: Warriors From the Magic Mountain* played an important role in the transnationalization and, for want of a better word, the "technologization" of Hong Kong cinema during the 1980s and 1990s.[3] It worked more than most other films of its moment to usher Hong Kong cinema in and through the age of postmodern culture, toward the age of digital composition, global sovereignty, and transnational flow. It is in that sense important to recall that *Zu: Warriors* was the first film produced locally in Hong Kong to employ Hollywood-based special effects talent directly, in sharp contrast to common subsequent perceptions of a primarily East-to-West labor migration. *Zu* may thus have paved the way for some of the most far-reaching changes in global popular culture of the 1990s, but not necessarily in the ways its makers may have expected or intended.

Of course, employment of such expensive forms of cultural labor within the confines of established Hong Kong studio hierarchies inflated the film's budget to unprecedented levels and helped to secure the film's notoriety as an especially high-profile instance of popular cinema as financial crisis during the inflation of Hong Kong's bubble economy in the1980s. But the bursting of that speculative bubble was also a productive event. The experience of making and being criticized for *Zu: Warriors* contributed no small part to Tsui Hark's desire to found and develop Film Workshop and Cinefex, his own personal efforts to modernize Hong Kong cinema. These independent institutions, while producing many of the definitive films of their time, pushed him ultimately towards small-batch, "boutique" production of digital visual effects for the sake of local and regional competition in world cultural markets.

Maybe it was inevitable, given *Zu's* place in the evolving conjuncture of forces in Hong Kong cinema, that in the late 1990s Tsui Hark would pursue the making of a digitized successor to *Zu:*

Warriors — the interesting but flawed *Legends of Zu* — at the same time that Hollywood was greedily absorbing Hong Kong action choreography into some of its most successful blockbusters. Nevertheless, it would be a mistake to equate *Zu: Warriors* purely and simply with the technoculture of globalizing capitalism. *Zu: Warriors From the Magic Mountain* also represented one of the earliest expressions of what Steven Teo and other scholars of the Hong Kong New Wave have described as Tsui's personal search for post-colonial identity in Hong Kong. That tendency came to its fullest fruition nearly a decade later in the *Once Upon a Time in China* series, where Hong Kong's autonomy blurred with a hopeful reading of Chinese national sovereignty. In comparison to that landmark series of films, *Zu: Warriors From the Magic Mountain* has received scant critical scrutiny. Through it, perhaps more so than most films by Tsui Hark, we can detect a strange new cultural alchemy, persistently articulating autonomous locality in the midst of the emergent transnational. In *Zu: Warriors*, technology and nationality, mythology and politics constantly interpenetrate and lend meanings to one another.

My aim in this book is to understand the ways that *Zu: Warriors* occupied a series of historical crossroads that have not yet been adequately connected. The tendencies represented by Tsui Hark's efforts on *Zu: Warriors*, and the later *Legend of Zu*, need to be placed among the most significant material and allegorical axes in the transformation of the Hong Kong action cinema during the late twentieth century. To put it in the baldest binary fashion, *Zu* both witnessed and leveraged Hong Kong cinema from its "territorialized" phase, focused on local identities, small-scale means of production, and an uneven mixture of optical and corporeal technologies, to its "deterritorialized" phase, associated with the production of transnational identities, global financing structures, and increasingly monolithic digital visual technologies.

The methodological approach of this book is to cover these

ideas from an interdisciplinary standpoint, integrating diverse contexts into a large framework for understanding the film's meanings. This book does not discuss separately the means of production and the plotting or content of the film, or concerns such as the performance of local and regional identities. Instead, it looks to describe points of mutual implication and interaction: to show how, for instance, technological transformation has been bound up at several points with the production of identity and the financing of culture. In that way we can re-describe *Zu: Warriors From the Magic Mountain* as a much more important film than it normally gets credit for within major narratives of the Hong Kong film industry, and even within depictions of Tsui's own career. The chapters have been organized in sequence to illustrate the film's aesthetic, political, economic, and technological navigation of the passage from postmodernism to globalism, or what Negri and Hardt have recently called "Empire." By thinking through these sorts of integrated critical frameworks we can begin to understand the real centrality of *Zu: Warriors From the Magic Mountain* to the transformation of commercial cinematic production in Hong Kong since the late-1970s, across the transnational networks that increasingly define both the limits and the possibilities of Hong Kong's locality.

Chapter 2 sets *Zu: Warriors From the Magic Mountain* within the context of Hong Kong's early-1980s political struggles over the formation of an "autonomous" post-colonial identity, in between British colonialism, Chinese nationalism, and capitalist globalism. I argue that the narrative of *Zu: Warriors* was an anticipatory act of social imagination. Its important intervention into the debates over Hong Kong's distinctive form of post-coloniality worked not by recovering images of an essential national subject but by imagining a more fluid and horizontal form of social order immanent to civil society itself. In doing so, *Zu* did not simply leap into the abyss of abstract cultural and political fantasy. It moved forward by looking backward. It revived the mythic form of the *wuxia* story as the means by which to look beyond the futures projected by the forces vying for control of Hong Kong in the early 1980s. Neither was this merely nostalgia. Tsui turned out *wuxia* tales with a twist. He sharply accentuated the genre's tendency to play with gender roles as a way to modernize the narrative and represent a self-conscious awareness of the problems presented by the pull within Hong Kong's cultural politics toward what we might call, following Akbar Abbas, the lures of localism, marginality, and cosmopolitanism. Standing between these tendencies, *Zu* staked an audacious bet on negation, ambivalence, and ambiguity. In that sense we might say that *Zu*'s subversive gender play literally became its anticipatory figure of Hong Kong's autonomous post-colonial identity.

Chapter 3 takes up the question of special effects technology and the connections between *Zu: Warriors* and popular Hollywood cinema of the late-1970s and early-1980s in the economic context of Hong Kong's "bubble economy." There is little question that *Zu* was lauded at the time primarily for its innovations in visual effects technology and its exploratory interfacing with international effects producers, having imported a number of prominent effects designers from the US. At the same time that special effects drove the film's budget skyward, they could not save it from financial disaster. *Zu: Warriors* became something of a cautionary parable for Hong Kong's film producers of the apparent dangers of speculative finance. The story did not end there though. For within the images produced by Tsui Hark for *Zu: Warriors* lay a fluid visual imagination far in advance of the dominant applications of special effects technologies at the time. By linking these technologies into new kinds of mixed technological economies, along with the more traditional forms of cinematic wire-work and Cantonese stage choreographies, *Zu: Warriors From the Magic Mountain* pre-visualized the continuous, highly mobile spatial imagination that defined the next stage of digital effects production and the increasingly cozy relationship between Hong Kong and Hollywood in the 1990s. It was, in all of these senses, both an example of the global postmodern and a glimpse beyond.

Chapter 4 looks beyond *Zu: Warriors* toward the fallout from its financial failure and its legacies for the newly technologized Hong Kong cinema of the 1990s. Initially, that fallout drifted toward Tsui Hark's new production company, Film Workshop, and its special effects production wing, Cinefex Workshop, founded in 1986. The success of Tsui's films made through Film Workshop gave him the opportunity to make significant technology purchases and to keep up with many of the changes in special effects design during the remarkable worldwide transition to digital compositing and 3-D animation in the early 1990s. At the same time, Hong Kong action cinema was discovered by Hollywood directors, effects producers, and cinematographers in search of a means to represent fluid martial choreographies commensurate to the newly mutable technologies of digital object design. This was a pathway already charted by Tsui Hark, although he was not given the credit he deserved for it. While many of his contemporaries aggressively deterritorialized their careers, becoming global stars, Tsui failed to catch on in Hollywood and veered back by the end of the 1990s to a re-exploration of the world he had conjured in *Zu: Warriors From the Magic Mountain*. By the end of the decade he had poured enough of his own resources back into Film Workshop and Cinefex that he could spearhead the making of a digital successor, *Legend of Zu*. On that film one can track the continuing changes in Tsui's perception of Hong Kong's post-coloniality as he veers back toward a re-imagination of the problem of transnational sovereignty in a way that has been articulated best by the recent work of Antoni Negri and Michael Hardt's concept of "Empire." At a moment when films like *Crouching Tiger, Hidden Dragon* and *The Matrix* seem to portend a final deterritorialization of Hong Kong's cinematic style, Tsui Hark's narratives and his means of production have offered significant, if not always immediately successful, alternative frameworks to imagine the dimensions and the drawbacks of Hong Kong's uneven patterns of post-coloniality amid the uncharted realms of transnational sovereignty.

2

Speeding Towards Autonomy:
Gender, *Wuxia,* and the Politics of Post-Coloniality in Hong Kong

[Hong Kong] has always been, and will perhaps always be, a port in the most literal sense — a doorway, a point in-between — even though the nature of the port has changed. A port-city that used to be located at the intersections of different spaces, Hong Kong will increasingly be at the intersections of different times or speeds.

- Akbar Abbas, *Hong Kong*[1]

The plot of *Zu: Warriors From the Magic Mountain* begins in chaos and ends in balance. Over a stunning wide shot of the sunrise from a beach that anticipates the opening images of *Once Upon a Time in China*, a narrator intones, "It is in the Fifth Century. China has been suffering from decades of civil war and unrest." As soon as these words are uttered the sunrise is replaced by a hard cut of rampaging horsemen riding off to battle. Soon, warriors from rival factions will unite to complete a mythic journey to contain and then to destroy an emergent evil force. In the process they seek to end the rivalries threatening to splinter China. Period narratives set in the midst of China's cyclic fragmentation have been commonplace throughout Tsui Hark's oeuvre. In *Zu: Warriors From the Magic Mountain*, as in the *Once Upon a Time in China* series, he emphasized repeatedly the necessity for some form of "national" Chinese cultural unity. *Zu: Warriors From the Magic Mountain* was, in that sense, a story about finding peace and building commonality out of fragmentation. Given its production and release schedule during the four-year period of negotiations leading up to the signing of the Hong Kong handover agreement between Great Britain and China, we might well argue that *Zu: Warriors* was a sort of anticipatory allegory of re-unification, an early call for post-colonial harmony staged in the vernacular dialect of Chinese mythology. One would not be entirely wrong to assume that was the case.

In the film's opening scene, the protagonist, a lowly military scout named Ti Ming-chi, is forced to choose between his two commanders who are arguing over whether to attack their enemies by water or by land. In an almost too-perfect allegory of Hong Kong's difficult position in between British and Chinese masters, the scout glances with alarm between the two of them and then bows his head, saying, "I will obey both your orders." This only enrages the generals. Panicked, Ti Ming-chi replies, "Then I will obey neither of your orders." One of the commanders yells, "That's worse! Kill him!" The compromised middle ground liquefies right before Ti Ming-chi's eyes. He flees from the raging armies as the troops follow in hot pursuit, and the opening battle is underway.

Yet, as with all great genre fictions, conflict and contradiction lie just beneath the surface of an otherwise simple story. *Zu: Warriors* was surely concerned with the question of Hong Kong's post-colonial identity, but not in any straightforward national-allegorical manner.[2] Many critics have noted the prevalence of apparently nationalist themes in Tsui Hark's films, yet almost none

Fig. 2.1 Ti Ming-chi bows before his two masters.

have been very precise about the nature and the form of Tsui's nationalism.[3] Rather than merely affirming the deep cultural unity of the Chinese nation, or asserting the putative uniqueness of Hong Kong's regional identity, *Zu: Warriors From the Magic Mountain* re-occupies the compromised middle ground in between. It stands at the crossroads of what Akbar Abbas has recently called the three "temptations" of Hong Kong's post-colonial identity politics: the local, the marginal, and the cosmopolitan.[4] While including symptoms of all, it was content with none. In retrospect, *Zu*'s formulation looks practically prescient for a world soon to be engulfed by the forces of cultural and financial globalization.

Like many of Hong Kong's young cultural workers coming of age professionally in the late-1970s, Tsui Hark became interested early in his career in the problem of Hong Kong's future political status.[5] Many have identified serious treatments of the problem of Hong Kong's political identity as one of the primary distinguishing features of the Hong Kong New Wave. Would Hong Kong ultimately be able to assert something like its own distinctive national identity, the most common form of anti-colonial identification, given the relatively unique conjunction between its ongoing post-industrial transition, its lack of a pre-colonial past, and its indeterminate political standing in between British and Chinese sovereignties? Would the category of nationality eventually threaten to swallow the territory whole within the vastness of China, even more than within the always incomplete and highly contested rule of the British Empire? How might the relative unevenness of their financial systems play out against the backdrop of those complicated international maneuvers? Would it become necessary to assert some sort of alternative identity category in response to the forces of unequal economic development in China and the ongoing articulation of Hong Kong's own distinctive version of Chinese nationality? All of these questions were unsettled and closely bound up with speculative public debates over the future terms and nature of Hong Kong's so-called regional "autonomy" — culturally, politically, and financially — under the auspices of a growing Chinese economy in the midst of post-Maoist market reforms but still absent any notably democratic political reforms.[6] *Zu: Warriors* almost inevitably took shape within shouting distance of those debates.

At the same time, another line of thinking ran through *Zu: Warriors From the Magic Mountain.* That other line suggests that appeals to nationality and the nation-state may have been inadequate solutions to Hong Kong's particular dilemmas. It was never made clear in *Zu: Warriors,* for instance, that the fractured nation-state might ever regain the ability to restore order over civil society. The restoration of order is never actually shown, and thus national closure is mostly forestalled. In its place, something like civil society itself, the bustling world of relations in between groups of non-state economic and political actors, might be installed as a new source of order. Social order might be transfigured horizontally throughout the social body, taken over by the actions and wills of ordinary people, rather than vertically through yet another incarnation of centralized state hierarchies.

Civil society as a form of sovereignty was necessarily as much a space of negation as it was of construction or assertion. The nature and the rules of such an immanent sovereign order were, and still are, mostly unclear. Nevertheless, anticipatory figures of an immanent, horizontal social order abounded in the film. That should be unsurprising in some ways given Hong Kong's long-standing reliance on dense networks of small entrepreneurialism for large portions of its internal regulation and economic growth. Even as the actual re-formation of social order and the termination of military conflict were withheld, the film concluded on the triumphal note that "the new generation must take over." Such phrasing had very specific meanings in the Hong Kong of the early 1980s given the uncertainty of the future role and composition of the local state during the process of transition. But its echoes did not stop at the borders of Hong Kong's territory. Calls for takeover by a new generation also related to ideas about similar changes in the role of the nation-state worldwide during the uneven transition to a new transnational form of capitalism whose circuits of exchange increasingly overflow and exceed the boundaries of any nation-state whatsoever. For, it was those global connections that framed much of the new generation's new cultural and political situation.

Hong Kong's distinctive urban and regional vantage point made the conceptual shift from anti-colonial nationalism to post-colonial globalism all the more tangible. Throughout the handover period Hong Kong's identity, as Ackbar Abbas describes it, remained quintessentially that of the port city, a space of constant political, economic, and cultural exchange. Thus, Hong Kong has remained an important location from which to map the material and imaginary transformation of contemporary sovereign spaces, whether strictly urban or national, into spaces for the regulation of high-speed trade and global flows of goods, money, people, and cultures, rather than spaces primarily for internal territorial demarcation. Abbas expands on the work of Anthony King, who argues that the colonial "gateway city" was the prototype for what Saskia Sassen later described as the urban control nexus of a rapidly globalizing financial capitalism, claiming that the remarkable thing about the handover period was not its roots in models of the colonial nation-state but its anticipation of "a form of governance that has no clear historical precedents."[7]

It is more correct to say that Tsui Hark was concerned in *Zu: Warriors* with an unusual project of anticipatory political imagination, one bound up with the tensions and necessities of local identity and clear preferences for civil forms of rule immanent to society, linked together with an understanding of Hong Kong's changing geo-strategic position as an emergent global city of speed, flow, transit, and temporality. To assert the existence of such a position, however, is not to say that it was altogether *realized*. Quite to the contrary, *Zu: Warriors From the Magic Mountain* was not reporting to its audiences on an already-completed transition. It was attempting to make large-scale historical changes both negotiable and actionable by making their contours and contradictions somehow socially imaginable. Its cultural tactics might best be described as providing unfinished imaginary resolutions to ostensibly real but highly abstracted political situations. *Zu: Warriors* thus undertook the virtually impossible task of visualizing the dilemmas of a rapidly changing postcolonial social order in advance of its realization by deferring the work of its social imagination onto ambivalent images of a mythic time-space and complex gendered identities. *Zu*'s broad-stroke deployment of Chinese mythology, updated by the refinements of Tsui Hark's high-speed editing style, imported Hollywood special effects, cleverly critical cultural feminism, and periodic outbursts of ironic self-awareness, were not simply uneven meeting grounds between East and West. The unusual conjunction of forms and forces provided essential materials for creating transitional and transformational images of a possible immanent social order without resolving into the foundations of yet another territorialized "nationalism." Riffing on the phrasing of Stephen Teo, we might say that rather than a territorialized version of Chinese national identity, *Zu: Warriors From the Magic Mountain* described the outlines of a new and highly mobile form of "autonomy on speed" for an emergent but unrealized post-colonial Hong Kong.[8]

Revisiting *Wuxia*

> The world of the *wuxia* is different from that of society. The *wuxia* operates in a realm under the surface of society and the rule of law, called *jianghu* — a world made up of individuals and their relationships, rather than the collective and the government.
>
> - Ang Lee, 2001

The genre of Chinese mythology that *Zu* both fit within and attempted to revise was the *wuxia* tale. According to David Bordwell, among many others, *wuxia* is a relatively old narrative form within the Chinese literary tradition, dating back at least to the ninth century AD. It means, literally, a story of the martial, chivalrous knight. Unlike the Japanese Samurai tradition, wherein the wielding of the sword was reserved specifically for members of the Samurai class, the hero of the *wuxia* tales was usually an unattached warrior, caught in between conflicting factions or warlords. They fought for right and justice ("*yi*") rather than for any particular power or side. Their concept of justice was situational. *Situational justice* meant that ethical dictates depended largely on context rather than universal principles, and could at times appear practically unethical depending upon one's point of view. The *wuxia* hero could thus adopt a kind of outlaw persona while at the same time claiming to act primarily out of principle.

Adding a further wrinkle to the formula, the *wuxia* hero,

unattached to any particular power, was bound by strict Confucian hierarchies. That potential internal conflict repeatedly produced splits between the characters' personal convictions and the demands of social hierarchy. Much of the generative ethical and narrative force of the *wuxia* tale can be traced to these sorts of divisions. For instance, the revenge plot that features so prominently in many *wuxia* stories has its roots not in simple vigilantism, but in honor and respect for the higher levels of a hierarchy (teacher, father, etc.) Rather than resolving easily into one side or another, virtually irresolvable conflicts between personal convictions and social demands lay at the root of *wuxia*'s tragic worldview. The struggles of the *wuxia* hero to act morally in the fallen world of chaos and social disorder pushed her (an unusually large number of *wuxia* heroes were female) toward becoming a form of order in and of herself, operating immanently to civil society rather than toward the construction or the imposition of a new form of state authority.

Wuxia tales were early favorites in the popular Chinese cinema emanating from the Shanghai studio system as early as the late-1920s. Their ubiquitous cinematic presence built off of their popularity in operatic and serial fictional forms during the nineteenth century. Throughout the mid-twentieth century, following the transfer of much of the Shanghai studio system to Hong Kong, until the early 1970s, they formed a staple core of Hong Kong's film production. That era of cinematic *wuxia* in Hong Kong reached its artistic high point with King Hu's epic meditation, *Touch of Zen*. Around that point, *wuxia* was largely superseded by the flood of "kung fu" films issuing from the breakthrough international success of Bruce Lee. In place of *wuxia*'s focus on archaic chivalric values, cultural authenticity, legendary or fantastical narratives and a focus on technologies of martial combat beyond the surface of the body itself (*wuxia* tales often contained a near-fetishistic focus on non-organic technologies of combat), kung fu, especially in Bruce Lee's terms, adopted a resolutely modern and international focus while centering its martial aesthetic on the supreme physical prowess of the solitary, male avenging hero.[9] To claim an absolute break between these two forms would be a serious error. Many kung fu films, even in the wake of Bruce Lee, took up mythic themes and emphasized the distinctive ethical code of the autonomous hero. The shift of film production in Hong Kong toward the kung fu film tended to undermine the popularity of the classic *wuxia* swordplay film while displacing theatrical wirework aesthetics, in favor of authentic physical skill, as the primary signifier of Hong Kong's action style worldwide. The rise of Jackie Chan's comedic kung fu masochism as the heir-apparent to Bruce Lee's stoic sadism only reinforced this overall tendency even as Chan reincorporated certain forms of operatic wirework into his ultra-realist stunts.

Although a number of counter-examples from the 1970s can be found, including Patrick Tam's *The Sword* and Tsui Hark's own successful TV serial, *The Gold Dagger Romance, Zu: Warriors From the Magic Mountain* flew in the face of the general drift of late-1970s and early-1980s Hong Kong action aesthetics by returning to an apparently faithful version of *wuxia*'s classical generic conventions. The plot of *Zu: Warriors* mostly follows the familiar *wuxia* arc, derived in this case from Huanzhu Louzhu's classic martial arts novel, *Swordsmen From the Zu Mountains*. As the film opens, in fifth-century China, warring armies are clashing over possession of Mount Zu, a key strategic location in the West. Tsui deploys a strikingly modernist primary-color contrast to signify the armies in conflict, allowing him to identify distinct forces with a minimum of verbal exposition. He also just as quickly introduces a sly sense of self-referential humor, repeated throughout the film, by having two of the soldiers declare in the midst of combat, "What a colorful battle this is!" That sense of ironic self-awareness forecasts the film's playful subversion of *wuxia*'s generic structure. However, the full dimensions of the film's subversive intent did not become entirely apparent until well into the story. The narrative launches us into the midst of the genre while at the same time telling us that we ought to be prepared to notice the generic and cinematic practices working upon us, establishing an internal pattern of play between surfaces and depths, comedy and tragedy, governance and resistance.

The film's protagonist, Ti Ming-chi, played by the dynamic martial artist Yuen Biao, is introduced as a bumbling scout for the West Zu army. Attacked by his own troops, he makes an impromptu alliance with an East Zu soldier. They cooperate to flee the scene of an almost farcical battle where the soldiers are identified by their striking red, yellow, green, blue, and orange uniforms. Alliances between the armies seems to shift almost from moment to moment, as red soldiers fight yellow then suddenly end up collaborating with the yellow armies against the blues or the greens. Helped by a push from his newfound friend, Ti Ming-chi plunges from a high cliff and careens into the depths of a mysterious canyon. He flees an impending lighting storm and soon finds himself descending deeper and deeper into a poorly lit cave. Suddenly he is attacked again, this time by a handful of malevolent creatures with glowing blue eyes. The creatures leap from urns and attack him from the air as if by magic. Ti Ming-chi resists but finds himself wrapped up by the creatures in a heavy cloth-like substance. He is on the verge of being killed when he cries out for his "Mommy!" and is saved by the unexpected appearance of a master swordsman dressed in brilliant white robes, named Ting Yin, played by Adam Cheng.

Ti Ming-chi begs Ting Yin to become his teacher and to return with him to the world of men to help end their ceaseless conflict, but Ting Yin refuses. Ting Yin expresses a deep resignation, saying that conflict between humans is perpetual and that Ti Ming-chi should go into seclusion in the mountains while he still can tell right from wrong. As it unfolds, Ting Yin's worldview is clearly not the position of the film as a whole. The remainder of the plot pushes Ting Yin increasingly out into the world, often against his better judgment or his will. Soon thereafter, the two of them are attacked again, this time by ethereal creatures named the "Blood Crows." At the same time, they encounter a monk named Hsiao Yu and his sidekick Yi Chen, played by Damian Lau and Mang Hoi. These two monks are also engaged in combat with the Blood Crows. At first, relations between the two pairs are contentious, with Hsiao Yu declaring that he doesn't need extra companions. But they decide to band together anyhow when Hsiao Yu relates his three-year quest to locate the Evil Disciples, an aim evidently shared by Ting Yin, and his intention to confront them immediately.

Ti Ming-chi and Ting Yin accompany Hsiao Yu and Yi Chen into the Evil Temple. A wild battle with the Disciples erupts, mixing both natural and supernatural elements, with the two masters and their apprentices flying frantically around the room even though they are outnumbered by their enemies. The four are soundly defeated, but not killed. They are forced to flee the temple. They argue over where the battle went wrong and agree to part ways. Almost immediately though, they find themselves pulled back together again and confronted with an even greater threat: the Blood Demon itself, a multi-horned embodiment of evil. Hsiao Yu is seriously wounded in battle. His condition is stabilized by the actions of Ting Yin, but only temporarily. The rest are only rescued from certain death by the appearance of Long Brows, an old wizard, played by Sammo Hung, who holds off the Blood Demon with his Sky Mirror. Long Brows can only hold off the Demon for 49 days, after which the Blood Demon will be unstoppable and evil will engulf the world. He tells the group that in order to prevent that from happening they must find and unite the Purple and Green Twin Swords, located on Heaven's Blade Peak.

The group of four sets out together, burdened with the magnitude of their quest. Ti Ming-chi laments aloud that, "The world is in more disarray than I thought. I had originally asked you to save us mortals. Now I can't tell who is saving who." Their immediate concern is the condition of Hsiao Yu, still poisoned from his encounter with the Blood Demon. At a rest stop by a cool pond Hsiao Yu sits placidly under a translucent white netting while Ti Ming-chi and Yi Chen playfully transgress Ting Yin's strict tutelage by gathering fish from the water to cook for their lunch. Their play is interrupted by the appearance of the Blood Demon's double on a ledge high above them, disguised as Ting Yin. At first they think he is angered about the fish, but realize otherwise when he attacks them by firing bolts of energy. The real Ting Yin suddenly reappears and fights off the double, which then mutates into an image of a woman dressed in brilliant red robes. Almost as soon as she appears, she is decapitated by Ting Yin's flying sword.

Setting off once again, their first destination is the Fort, a stronghold of female warriors governed by the magical Countess, played by Brigitte Lin, to find a healer for Hsiao Yu. At first they are denied their request by the women warrior-healers who tend the Fort. Hsiao Yu's wounds are so deep that only the Countess herself can heal them. The Countess will see only those patients whom Fate has prescribed. The test of Fate is a small blue flame that burns only for a short time each day. If the flame burns out before the Countess appears then Fate will have spoken and Hsiao Yu will not be healed. Ting Yin attempts to intervene directly in Fate by reaching into the flame, extracting it and trying to control it to call the Countess. The women of the Fort are stunned by his audacious attempt to circumvent Fate. His plan works though: the Countess appears. Strangely, she looks exactly like the woman in red who appeared as the mutated form of the Blood Demon's double. Ti Ming-chi calls her a witch. The Countess, angered, retaliates against him with deadly force. Ti Ming-chi becomes badly wounded. Ting Yin must attempt to revive him on his own. A bizarre sequence ensues where Ting Yin re-molds Ti Ming-chi's body like a piece of modeling clay, infusing his energy into him while Ti Ming-chi looks comically flabbergasted at the elasticity of his flesh.

The Countess finally agrees to heal Hsiao Yu in an elaborate ceremony conducted in a chamber lined with mobile Buddhist statues. She succeeds, but is exhausted by the effort. She falls from the air, only to be caught by Ting Yin. At first she is angered, slapping him in the face. Later, she reconsiders and engages in an extended flirtation with Ting Yin, capped by the two of them prancing around her chambers on animated stone animal statues. Then suddenly, after having left the Countess's protection, Ting Yin is possessed by the Blood Demon after he attempts to offer a sword to Ti Ming-chi. They return to the Fort to heal him, but the Countess refuses to help him fight this greater evil. This time, the flame of Fate has gone out. Ting Yin tells Ti Ming-chi that as his disciple he is bound by the rules of their order to kill him and rid him of the evil possession. Ti Ming-chi draws his sword and charges his master, but fakes the strike. Pulling back, he yells to the assembled crowd, "To hell with fate and principles, we're letting a man die because of a flame!" The Countess agrees to help treat him and nearly sacrifices herself, but finds herself ultimately powerless against the possession. Ting Yin is not healed. To contain him and his demon in the Fort the Countess breaks her Ice Mirror and freezes the Fort along with everyone inside. Ti Ming-chi and Yi Chen are helped to escape by Chi Wu-shuang, a young female warrior.

The three of them are left with no other choice but to set out on their own, without the help of their masters, to recover the Twin Swords. Claiming that the Blood Demon was allowed to get his way in the first place because their masters refused to work together, they make a pact between them not to repeat the mistakes of the past. They form a unified fellowship. Arriving at Heaven's Blade Peak their first encounter is with Heaven's Blade, the guardian of the border between good and evil. He has chained himself to a large, spherical stone because his body has been invaded by an evil force and the only way for him to remain as guardian is to restrain his actions. Nevertheless, the border is weakening and the battle against the Blood Demon must be completed before it collapses and even the Twin Swords will not be able to prevail. Heaven's Blade shows them the way to the keeper of the swords just as Ting Yin reappears, now fully taken over by the Blood Demon. A battle erupts between Ting Yin and Heaven's Blade. During the chaos Ti Ming-chi is cast across the border into the evil territory, only to be saved by Yi Chen, who goes in after him. They are rescued from the evil territory by Heaven's Blade, who sacrifices himself so that they might escape.

At last, on top of the Peak, they encounter Lady Li I-chi, the keeper of the swords. She gives them to Ti Ming-chi and Yi Chen, along with strict instructions regarding the exact way in which they must be unified to fight the Blood Demon. She poses them with a paradox, that the two swords are strongest when they unite, yet they must not touch one another. Confessing that she has never been able to solve this paradox she contacts Long Brows for the solution. Long Brows tells her that the swords may be united only when the swordsmen "have the same mind."

As the two apprentices attempt to leave the Peak they are confronted by the possessed Ting Yin, who uses his powers to keep them from uniting the swords. They battle Ting Yin, yet separately they are no match for him. Meanwhile, the armies of East and West Zu are about to resume fighting. Long Brows attempts to hold on to his control but his strength fails him. The Blood Demon is nearly freed from the Sky Mirror as Ting Yin interposes himself between the Twin Swords. In the end though, the swords are united when the Countess suddenly appears and sacrifices herself by colliding with Ting Yin, saying to herself that she and Ting Yin "will be together in another world." The Blood Demon is finally defeated. Ti Ming-chi and Yi Chen return to the armies they fled at the story's beginning to attempt the unification of diverse forces on earth realm as well as the supernatural realm. Tsui Hark himself has a momentary cameo as a soldier in blue, fighting against the soldier in red who originally helped to save Ti Ming-chi. The fighting continues, but the protagonists announce an impending era of perpetual peace if "all minds are in unison." They leap into the air together as the camera freeze-frames on the soldier's body in mid-spring out of frame, almost as if in distant reply to Bruce Lee's famous freeze-frame leap at the lens to close out *Fists of Fury*.

Playing With Orientalism

> I think that identity is a product of the will, not something given
> by nature or history.
> - Edward Said, Out of Place: A Memoir

Zu: Warriors From the Magic Mountain cleared conceptual space for its preferred form of power and social order through a series of subversive visual and narrative moves. This series of subversions, in some ways paralleling the quest of the characters themselves, passed through a sequence of narrative gateway points, or key moments when the narrative forced transformational choices on its characters, each time negating prior conditions of the characters. To a certain extent this was to be expected from the outlines of the "quest" narrative, yet unlike many quests in which the goal is achieved but the characters remain fundamentally unchanged, *Zu*'s emphasis always remained on the side of transformation over continuity.

The film's "gateways" ushered the characters along through the story, but not in any neutral way. Each passage led to a point of gendered social exchange. Each passed through women (the Fort, the Countess and Lady Li I-chi) or through feminized men (the "virgin" hero Ti Ming-chi and the chained and demoralized gatekeeper, Heaven's Blade). This placed *Zu: Warriors From the Magic Mountain* squarely in line with Tsui Hark's most repeated social and aesthetic concerns. As Lisa Morton perceptively notes,

"The one motif to appear most frequently in the Tsui Hark oeuvre is that of feminine power."[10] Subversively feminized subjects which refuse to cede their social power based upon their gender — subjects given in part by the generic contours of the *wuxia* tale itself — served as the hinges for *Zu*'s images of an autonomous Hong Kong identity emerging from in between British and Chinese nationalities, in direct relation to an emerging logic of world order based upon high-speed, cross-border cultural and financial flows. In effect, the film's feminized subjects occupied the affirmative and productive imaginary location of Hong Kong's ongoing post-colonial and post-industrial transformations. They were, in the broadest sense, allegorical models of the film's concept of autonomy.

Just as often as the gateway characters were sexed female, they were given to subversive play with familiar masculine identities regardless of their actual sexed bodies. Other times, the characters actually switched their sexed bodies while retaining their previous gendered voices. Many of the film's female characters were able to play out variations on masculine identities while retaining significant elements of their feminine performances. At the same time, typical male-bonding rituals constantly failed. Relations of fate, hierarchy, and tradition repeatedly fell prey to acts of will and desire, forcing open gateways in the story that might otherwise have remained closed. The film's protagonists, warriors in their own rights, were pictured as comically feminized, even de-sexualized men. At all points in the narrative a clear preference was expressed for movement and passage across boundaries of self and geography rather than for stasis, conservation, and centrality. Tsui spent his generous semiotic surplus with liberal abandon. Each of the film's gendered encounters thus contained possibilities for role reversal, inversion and even, in the end, virtual inhabitation of alternate sexed bodies. "Feminization," in this sense, was construed within *Zu: Warriors* both as a liberatory cultural tactic and as a broad allegorical framework, not as a pejorative social judgment.

Tsui's playfully perverse gendered images alternately inverted and turned inside out the stereotypically feminized and Orientalized Western images of Chinese subjectivity. As Edward Said once described it, the discursive logics of the Western colonial Empires feminized the "Orientalist" subject through a, "flexible, positional superiority, which puts the Westerner in a whole series of positive relations with the Orient without ever losing him the relative upper hand."[11] That kind of positional superiority was a deeply gendered affair, based upon parallel logics of dominance and subordination, activity and passivity. *Zu: Warriors* attempted to rewrite these ambiguous subject positions as the positive ethical bases for Hong Kong's post-colonial and post-industrial revisions of social subjectivity. It did so, however, without repeating the contours of the anti-colonial inversions that marked so many earlier responses to colonization and to Orientalism. The condition of post-coloniality in Hong Kong was thus imagined as a creative condition, or a space for genuine innovations in the self, pictured in part through the film's gendered transformations. By daring to play with the colonial Orientalist imaginary in these ways, setting him apart strikingly from a figure like Bruce Lee's more muscular anti-colonialism, Tsui was able to produce a range of sensuously imaginary spaces and fluidly ambiguous social identities that were no longer strictly beholden to any essential polarities of the past.

In the final instance, successful self images within *Zu: Warriors* were ones that negated conditions imposed by the past, or, at the more abstract level, conditions imposed by the genre, in order to act according to their senses of duty and desire. On the one hand this was in keeping with the limits of *wuxia*, with its traditions of unaligned heroism and self-sacrifice. On the other hand, the film chafes at those limitations and seeks to overcome them by playing at subversion of the self, even to the point of risking identification at times with something resembling the Orientalist imaginary. In either case, to read *Zu: Warriors From the Magic Mountain* as an anticipatory allegory of Hong Kong's mutating social identity in the age of globalizing capitalism, receding colonialism and post-Maoist Chinese nationalism, such a reading must pass through the film's feminized gateway points.

We start to pass through these almost from the opening moments of the story. When Ti Ming returns the enemy Red Army soldier's water bottle to him, thereby ending their conflict, they lament to each other that their conversation must remain necessarily a moment out of time given the violent context of battle and the unreasoning passions involved. Nevertheless, despite their insights, they agree to help each other evade the encroaching combat, and in that sense successfully buck the dead hand of Fate that seeks to drive them apart with the wedge of non-reflexive antagonistic identification. The water bottle itself, which returns at the conclusion of Ti Ming-chi's journey, is a symbol of the mutual exchange between them, a token of care and concern over the destructive force of the battlefield. In a more sentimental key, one might say it exemplifies an ethic of friendship as a horizontal exchange in place of the typically masculine hierarchies of martial valor. Their cowardly act of fleeing the scene, an act that is overtly feminized in the context of the high-volume bellicosity of the warring armies, becomes the lever that sends Ti Ming-chi plunging toward the subterranean world where he confronts the unexpected threat of the Blood Demon.

When he arrives in the subterranean world, only to be confronted and captured by the mysterious blue-eyed creatures from the urns, Ti Ming-chi plaintively cries out for his "Mommy!" It is this cry, and not the threat of imminent danger to his person per se, that prompts the sudden arrival of Ting Yin as his savior in white. The relationship between these two men was comically feminized from the start in terms of the relation of a mother to her child. Clearly this part of their relationship was intended for laughs, much like Ti Ming-chi's subsequent moniker of "virgin boy" (which, not coincidentally, saved him once again from attack) but there is very little indication that this laughter was meant altogether unseriously. In fact, there is good reason to believe that these jokes, beyond their humor, laid the groundwork for film's somewhat more remarkable exercise in failed male-bonding and mentorship. In this key area *Zu: Warriors* breaks with traditions of the classic *wuxia* form and begins to articulate its own idiosyncratic vision.

In *Zu: Warriors*, the standard relations of master and apprentice, apparent throughout *wuxia*, are continually deferred and deformed. Unlike, say, the films of John Woo, where male bonding is understood practically as a transcendent ethical form, hailing like a wind from the archaic past to clear the stagnant and corrupted modern atmosphere, *Zu: Warriors* cites, then interrupts, these bonds at almost every turn. This is not to say that Tsui configured masculine bonding somehow as being an undesirable relationship. To the contrary, much of the plot turns on the deep-seated desires of all the primary male characters for some sort of intimate homosocial experience. As Gayatri Spivak would say, male homosociality is a relationship that the characters "cannot not desire," at least in part because of their placement inside the constraints of genre and history. Yet, the film nevertheless places male homosociality "under erasure," by refusing it the completion it seeks.[12] In part, this happens through the resignification of paternal bonds of male authority into mirrored maternal bonds of caring and concern. Maternalism itself, however, was undermined by its re-signification as a comedic form of gender switching. Its unresolved overlay onto the generic frame of masculine bonding maintained a form of doubled vision. At all the key gateway points in the narrative we can perceive both the sign of male homosocial desire and the mark of its erasure.

Ting Yin begins his journey as the reluctant master, and Ti Ming-chi as the overeager apprentice. When Ti Ming-chi asks him outright to accept him as a student he is immediately rebuffed. Ti

Ming-chi is persistent though, pressing Ting Yin on multiple occasions for his acceptance. Finally, when Ting Yin agrees to arm Ti Ming-chi by offering him the sword that would be given to an apprentice, were he to take one on, the Blood Demon "infects" Ting Yin and forces the group back to the Fort once again to seek the services of the Countess. Once again, much like Hsiao Yu's attempted offer of the beads signifying mastery of his clan, resulting in their being snapped apart by the bumbling student, exchange between men has been forestalled. Ting Yin's sword, the literal sign of their attempted paternal exchange, has been corrupted and is unable to complete the deal. Before they depart, under extreme duress, Ting Yin accepts Ti Ming-chi as his student in reality, not merely performatively, but only to find himself submerged once more beneath the weight of the Blood Demon's will and thereby rendered impotent, or unable to act even in his own defense. His impotence in this moment leads Ti Ming-chi and Yi Chen on their final quest for the Twin Swords without the benefit of paternal guidance. Ting Yin's failure pushes them toward psychic redefinition, coming into selfhood as autonomous subjects above and beyond the dictates of the master-apprentice dynamic.

From a somewhat different angle, the character of the Countess also articulated the logic of autonomous identity in and through the shifting lens of her gendered selfhood. She began the narrative as the magical ruler of a hidden city of women, a sort of warrior high-priestess, and ended up the exemplar of heroic sacrifice by hurling her body at Ting Yin to allow the union of the Twin Swords and the completion of the quest. One might well say her character exemplified from the outset a modern variant on certain very old tropes of exclusive feminine power. She might appear by definition as an important but insufficient overture towards contemporary feminist ideals within what can seem to be an endless litany of troubling portraits of women in Hong Kong action cinema. David Bordwell argues as much when he claims that, "Women suffer terribly in most [Hong Kong] action films, a circumstance not offset by the woman-warrior tradition."[13] Yet there is more to the Countess than merely the making of positive images of powerful women. The performance of her play between available forms of selfhood alternately determined by Fate and by Will is in many ways the linchpin to the film's concept of autonomous identity.

When the male protagonists arrive at the Fort and are confronted by the restrictive practices of the female warrior-healers, they refuse to submit to Fate's commands by keeping alive the blue flame that permits access to the Countess. They are literally feminized by the Fort's female gatekeepers who identify themselves with the tripwire mechanism of Fate. The same mechanism of Fate keeps the Countess trapped within her chambers and subject to the call of the outside world, even if only for a limited duration. In part, her attraction to Ting Yin stemmed from his willingness to violate the rigid social formalities of the Fort. His seizure of the flame and his outright negation of Fate brought her rushing from her chambers. Yet, her first instinct is not to take up the mantle of the caregiver. Instead, she defends her integrity against the apprentices' cries that she resembles the witch they have just fled. Her attack is an act of integrity whose ultimate meaning is secured when Ting Yin admonishes the students not to "call every woman you see a witch." Their reply to his mannerly pedagogy is equally genuine, that she did in fact appear identical to the witch they saw transformed before their eyes. The truth of these relations lies elsewhere. The visual is not the entire circumference of the self. The female body of the Countess, clearly an object for the cinematic gaze, nevertheless evades any simple reduction to any particular identity category. Her second appearance, placing the visual fetish of the female body in quotations, exceeds the frame of her visual limitations, pushing toward a modern concept of the ethical self as an abstraction defined by its actions rather than its physicality or its traditional constraints.

The figure of the Countess exceeds the boundaries of Fate's traditional opposition to modernity. Rather than the Orientalist binaries between tradition and modernity, passivity, and activity, passed down to the present via modernization theory and "development" discourse, the Countess signifies subversive play between times and speeds as much as she merges gendered identity positions into an image of an alternate ethical framework for post-colonial Hong Kong. Her act of self-sacrifice, literally merging herself with the body of Ting Yin into a new whole, while casting them both toward "the next world," is a much larger act than an act for herself alone. At once an individual act of merger with the object of her desire, the achievement of her deferred union with Ting Yin, and a social act of self-determination, allowing humanity to determine its own fate and to resist the encroachment of evil in the guise of the Blood Demon, her act also signifies an image of temporal circularity and subjective reincarnation, tipping forward and backward simultaneously. This is, in that sense, not merely the triumph of modern desires for autonomous self-determination. Better, it is the refusal of autonomous selfhood as merely a modern form, finding instead the source materials of a new individuality simultaneously rooted in the past and projected toward the future, across the limit conditions of gender, time, myth, and Fate.

Neither Local, Nor Marginal, Nor Cosmopolitan

> There is one essential condition ... that must be there if the postcolonial subject is not to be reabsorbed and assimilated: it must not be another stable appearance, another stable identity.
> - Ackbar Abbas, *Hong Kong*

Zu: Warriors placed the Orientalist worldview under erasure by playfully negating the limits of the gendered subject that formed its foundations. From the ruins of that negation emerged images of new, unbounded, autonomous subjects, hailed by the voices of the "new generation" that the film cries out for in the end. And yet, one is left at the end of *Zu: Warriors* with a vague sense of dissatisfaction, as if the film had somehow failed to close the circle and disclose the positive contents of its characters and its ideas. There was, for instance, a palpable if clichéd sense that internecine conflict should come to an end and that ordinary people will need to take Fate into their own hands rather than resting content with the strictures of hierarchy and tradition at the same time that they draw upon the narrative resources of tradition as a way of measuring the limits of their departures and saving them from pure abstraction. That was a rather thin assertion though, overlaying a much larger sense of absence and evasion. Within the *wuxia* genre it was commonplace for protagonists to refuse worldly closure by adhering to a transcendent ethics over and above the cluttered antagonisms of the State. Perhaps some of *Zu*'s stubborn refusal of closure might also be attributed to the formal legacy of *wuxia* as popular serial fiction. Still, there seems to be an especial emptiness to its conclusion, with nothing really being concluded and the elements of its possible alternatives being defined mostly by what they are not.

In that context, Ackbar Abbas's insistent negation of the concepts of locality, marginality, and cosmopolitanism in recent Hong Kong cultural politics might prove to be a useful guide toward a reframing of the meanings of *Zu*'s curious absences. As Abbas puts it, taking up each one in turn, "the difficulty with the local is in locating it ... particularly tricky in a place like Hong Kong, with its significant proportion of refugees, migrants and transients." The local, or the authentic traditions upon which a post-colonial Hong Kong identity might be founded, has been confounded by Hong Kong's placement within global patterns of population flow. The strategy of marginality founders on being stabilized as a token of identity and difference within larger fields of power, thus merely an "avant-garde romance." The cosmopolitan strategy falls short as well, on the grounds that it tends toward an over-optimistic universalism, one that smears the shadings of genuine otherness and unequal power relations with the rosy dreams of a unified world culture.[14] For Abbas, these are all general tendencies of the postcolonial condition that contain specific relevance for Hong Kong given its placement at the intersections of decolonization, global finance, and urbanism, and the long-term problem of its identity and difference within the wider frame of Chinese national and diasporic cultures. There are for him, no particular resolutions to be had for these conjunctions, except to build upon the ground cleared by negation itself. In that sense, he shares much in common with Tsui Hark's work on *Zu: Warriors*. Much like the complex and ambiguous gendered identities of its characters, Tsui Hark took note of possible desires for each of these tendencies, but he aligned himself with none of them, leaving behind instead the marks of erasure and the pleasures of ambivalence in place of more positive or definitive enunciations of its aims.

Localism is perhaps the easiest strategy to discern, and also the easiest to criticize. Localism shows up in *Zu: Warriors* in the very conception of the film's production, its importation of Western culture labor to Hong Kong rather than the more common movement in later years from Hong Kong to the West — to a certain extent, remaking Hollywood in a Cantonese dialect. Yet, not only could the very same production concerns just as easily be interpreted the other way around, such intermixtures seem to lend themselves much more readily to descriptions of hybridity and transnational linkages than to mere "localization." On that point we merely find gestures of ambivalence. Recovering the narratives of *wuxia* might also be construed as a localist gesture, a version of the search for authentic local traditions upon which to base a post-colonial identity. Yet even within the film the characters constantly criticize *wuxia*'s generic conventions and expectations. In other ways, the film's travel narrative, keeping the plot constantly in motion between spaces, seems to lend itself to a diasporic, traveling notion of Chinese identity much more so than it does to a territorial version of locality.

In the same terms, concepts of the marginal appear to be a poor fit with *Zu*'s narrative concerns. In *Zu*, demands to engage the world always override desires for withdrawal. For instance, Ting Yin's tragic worldview and his insistence on remaining apart from the corrupted world of men comes under repeated assault by Ti Ming-chi, who asks on more than one occasion, "What good is knowing kung fu?" if one is unwilling to use those skills to help others in need? He demands that Ting Yin enter into the world rather than remaining aloof. Likewise, the failure of Ting Yin to cooperate with Hsiao Yu, and vice versa, leads directly to their strategic failure to defeat the Blood Demon. In order to move forward in the narrative the characters must come to terms with some form of social coordination. When Ting Yin cannot, he is infected (figuratively and literally) and ultimately made into an adversary that must be defeated. Marginality, pictured as a high-minded but ultimately myopic "go it alone" strategy, is therefore doomed to failure.

The inadequacies of localism and marginality would seem to leave open the cosmopolitan strategy as a plausible third outlet. There is little question that Tsui Hark brought some form of critical cosmopolitanism to his work, at least in the form of interconnection with world cinematic and political concerns. He was, after all, educated in the United States for a time and had worked with Third World Newsreel in New York City during the 1970s. Likewise, the film's visual style arcs toward recognition within the emerging transnational special effects community. Yet, his cosmopolitanism was shot through at almost all points with a sense that global universalism contains irresolvable contradictions, dissolving the palpable realities of difference, which inevitably lead one back to the inadequate localist and marginalist strategies. To that extent, one might say that the film's figure of cosmopolitanism was none other than the Blood Demon, the image of singular world dominion. The Blood Demon is the only character with that global ambition. In fact, when the Evil Disciples of the Blood Demon attack Ti Ming-chi and his compatriots in the beginning they announce that the only ones they will spare are those that agree with them. This statement forms the only overt testament within the film to the will of the Blood Demon to overrun all borders. Simply put, the story of the film as a whole is about the rush to shore up an inadequate local border, Long Brows's Sky Mirror, before the border itself is abolished and the world, not China alone, is taken over by the principle of global singularity and homogeneity, allegorized as the evil of the Blood Demon. At least in this sense, cosmopolitanism is held up as a fruitful but ultimately inadequate concept in need of significant modification through the inclusion of the insistently particular voices and "borders" of those most at risk of being silenced by the overtones of cultural universalism.

Although *Zu: Warriors* adopted neither locality, nor marginality, nor cosmopolitanism, it was not lacking the outlines of a conception of Hong Kong's political identity. At the heart of the film lay the contested middle ground upon which the immanent relations of civil society, in the shape of *wuxia*'s autonomous subjects, unbounded by Fate and unobstructed by universality, might articulate an new social order. That new order remained just beyond the final lip of the narrative. Perhaps prefiguring Abbas's admonition that the post-colonial subject ought not be simply another stable identity, *Zu: Warriors* refused narrative closure in the final instance. In its place was a gamble on negation, emblematized by the blurred leaping figure of the film's final image, rushing full speed towards an anticipated but as-yet undefined social autonomy.

3

Uneven Developments:
Optical Effects, Cinematic Space, and Hong Kong's Bubble Economy

Now this free-floating capital, on its frantic search for more profitable investments, will begin to live its life in a new context; no longer in the factories and the spaces of extraction and production, but on the floor of the stock market, jostling for more intense profitability, but not as one industry competing with another branch, nor even one productive technology against another more advanced one in the same line of manufacturing, but rather in the form of speculation itself: spectres of value, as Derrida might put it, vying against each other in a vast world-wide disembodied phantasmagoria.

- Frederic Jameson, *The Cultural Turn*[1]

According to the influential Hong Kong filmmaker and cultural critic Evans Chan, Hong Kong cinema has borrowed liberally from Hollywood for quite some time. "For the past two decades," he argues, "the Hong Kong film industry, never encumbered with a high-modernist tradition, has borrowed left and right from Hollywood movies to keep up its frenzied output."[2] Such extensive cultural borrowing, in the absence of the friction of "high modernism," has worked out well for the industry economically. At the same time, it has pushed mainstream Hong Kong cinema towards an embrace of the common international tropes of "postmodernism." As his main examples Chan notes the ubiquitous narrative pastiche, such as *Naked Killer*'s recycling of the plot to *Basic Instinct*, and the formal pastiche, such as *A Chinese Ghost Story*'s appropriation of the special effects shots from *Poltergeist*. In the latter case he could have just as easily been talking about *Zu: Warriors From the Magic Mountain*.

The postmodern elements of pastiche lay in its positioning between the original and the copy. Works of pastiche tend towards a version of Jean Baudrillard's definition of the "simulacra," or the copy without an original.[3] In the work of pastiche, cultural fragments are reorganized and recomposed without particular attention to their original meanings and contexts, into new forms bearing the surface traces of earlier fragments that are no longer necessarily connected to any point of origin. Intertextual connections are no longer citational but merely stylistic. The fragment becomes an overlay, playfully reciting forms of the past largely emptied of their contents. The work of pastiche thus has little use for concepts like originality, authorship, or authenticity insofar as the basic materials of the new work are the predigested fragments of previous works.

In Frederic Jameson's rather heavy-handed formulation, the rising international predominance of pastiche aesthetics has tended toward an evolving aesthetic of "blank parody," or the purely commercial spectacle.[4] Blank parody, with a strong odor of cultural nostalgia, rose to prominence in the West during the Reagan-Thatcher repudiation of neo-Keynesian social economics. In this new condition, just coming online as an articulated social order throughout the advanced capitalist world during the early 1980s, the universal triumph of exchange-value, realized through intensified international competition between large, debt-laden corporate culture industries, tended to erase even the memory of contextual origins for increasingly media saturated audiences. Cultural fragments became detached and free-floating in the new fast-paced, always-on global mediasphere, where TV re-runs jostled for time perpetually on a undifferentiated screen along with news and documentaries, Hollywood blockbusters, Japanese monster movies, British music videos, and Hong Kong action films. Still, residual traces of the fragment persisted. Its origins were always potentially retrievable, although not socially preferred, in the ghostly after-images of the postmodern pastiche. Jameson understood this new social order as a break with older forms of modern industrial cultural production, labeling it alternately "Late Capitalism," speculative financial globalization, or the "phantasmagoria" of free-floating, worldwide "specters of value."

The concept of a social and economic "phantasmagoria," indeed of finance capital itself as possessing a phantasmagoric structure, is an exceptionally provocative idea for film criticism, cultural theory, and political economy. By taking note of the roles played by the actual phantasmagoria in proto-cinematic, and even immersive, proto-simulational aesthetic developments during nineteenth century Western Europe, we might say that the so-called condition of "postmodernity" itself might be usefully described as a kind of globally extensive, socially immersive virtual space or "special effect."[5] The increasingly weightless and depthless forms of global space, perceived at least from the standpoint of the citizen-consumers of the advanced capitalist world, might then be understood as a new kind of incessantly mutating yet tightly controlled space of social simulation.[6] In this new phantasmagoric social space, production becomes detached from its referents in geography, political-economic relations likewise detached from the territorial state, as capital seeks to redefine global territory as a flat plane of mobility, always pushing against long-term entanglements in any specific form of worldly embodiment. In those terms, global space may appear more and more like a pure phantasmagoric abstraction, visualized nowhere apart from the spectral world of the undifferentiated screen.

Nevertheless, the historic rise of the global postmodern, as both dominant style and social formation, did not occur along a smooth cultural surface. The most interesting part of Chan's addendum to Jameson, writing that the postmodern in Hong Kong cinema stretches back farther than might ordinarily be assumed for the popular cinemas of the West, is that the tendency within Hong Kong cinema towards the postmodern pastiche was actually integral to the industry on a local level in a way that was largely autonomous from Hollywood's competitive interests. The growth of Hong Kong cinema's commercial pastiche aesthetics, borrowing or pirating from Hollywood's stock of valuable software, was primarily motivated in the 1970s and 1980s by internal competitive factors during a stage of the industry's development that was marked by unevenly developed economic and cultural relations between Hong Kong and Hollywood. There were important exceptions to this rule, related in most cases to the basic unpredictability of high-speed cross-cultural flows. But, until as late as the early 1990s the Hong Kong film industry saw very little need to compete head-on with Hollywood. Having already dominated the Southeast Asian regional market, in conjunction and competition with Japan, having cornered the networks of urban theatrical exhibition throughout the world's Chinatowns, and having largely resisted the inroads of Hollywood into the local consumer market in Hong Kong through the calculated emergence in the early 1970s of a popular Cantonese language film tradition, the Hong Kong film industry became a standard-bearer for autonomous cinematic cultures everywhere. Such images of standard-bearing cultural autonomy have led critics like Evans Chan to describe the decline of Hong Kong cinema's economic fortunes in the late-1990s as a loss not just to Hong Kong, but to world culture in general, being ground under the hoof beats of the global Hollywood rampage.

The basic problem with this periodization, despite Chan's and Jameson's compelling grand narratives, is that it privileges Hollywood as the ultimate source of the originals subsequently fragmented and recycled through the high-speed channels of Hong Kong's culture industries. It replicates something like a core-periphery theory of colonialism in glossy pop cultural terms. Yet, to what degree is it actually possible or desirable to argue that films like *Basic Instinct* and *Poltergeist* were actually original versions of anything more than Hollywood's own conceptions of their copyrights? When Chan rounds out the crescendo of his ever-more apocalyptic analysis by detecting the detritus of cultural decline and the triumph of commodity logic in the turn from pastiche to nostalgia in popular Hong Kong films of the 1990s, it is hard to figure out exactly what he means, given that many popular Hong Kong films of the past two decades have already contained multiple layers of cinematic pastiche and nostalgia, each drinking deeply from the well of cultural fragmentation. Even Frederic Jameson claims that a film like George Lucas's *Star Wars* already deployed pastiche aesthetics on multiple levels. In that particular case, 1930s serials melted with 1940s war films, 1950s westerns, and Japanese samurai epics in a cultural soup of immersive wide-screen spectacle. When Tsui Hark deployed the technologies and even part of the stylistic mythos of that so-called original, he was, at the very least, *making a pastiche of a pastiche.* If the originals themselves were already remade from a host of prior fragments, then to what degree might we reasonably criticize Hong Kong cinema's turn to pastiche in political terms?

Should we, in those terms, think of Tsui Hark's *Zu: Warriors From the Magic Mountain* as a kind of cultural Trojan Horse, making Hong Kong cinema safe for postmodern, global Hollywood's big-budget special effects blockbusters? Or, was Tsui using pastiche more self-consciously and tactically in the context of emerging possibilities for a new transnational commercial culture where Hollywood's output was only one node among many? There are good reasons to answer both yes and no to these questions. They are not inherently contradictory nor does the latter's insistence on the value of transnational culture necessarily preclude a critical discussion of transnationalism in the former. In fact, they may simply be different versions of the same basic problem: the drastic changes in global cultural markets prompted by Hollywood's increasingly aggressive international sales, advertising, and technology profile. *Zu: Warriors From the Magic Mountain* can be understood as both a symptom of and an attempted solution to that problem. Either way, it anticipated the problems posed by the reconstruction of Hollywood's technical and industrial structures well before the Hong Kong film industry as a whole confronted the dimensions of this fast-approaching crisis. Rather than dwelling on the coming crisis, it offered an alternative escape route by reframing the postmodern pastiche as an anticipatory tactic of cultural transnationalization. It sought to evade the Hollywood juggernaut by using selective mimicry and strategic mutations of the visual field.[7] *Zu: Warriors From the Magic Mountain* simultaneously incorporated and looked beyond the aesthetic habits of the social postmodern, towards new ways of imagining and living within the societies of postmodernity.

Janus-faced cultural strategies had been familiar to Tsui Hark from the beginning of his career. Keeping track of many different genres, styles, and cultural tendencies, without ever grounding himself in any one of them, had long been one of his signatures. In that sense he should have been quite at home with the films of George Lucas and Steven Spielberg. Beyond their insatiable culture-mulching and their often alarming tendencies towards proto-fascistic forms of mythic futurism, Tsui Hark never lost track of their potential aesthetic and industrial lessons. Having been trained in film school in the United States during the late-1960s, he was well positioned to observe the wholesale restructuring of Hollywood cinema precipitated in part by their films' event-scale releases and overwhelming economic profiles. Upon returning to the post-Bruce Lee Hong Kong cinema, of the emergent New Wave and the ascendant Jackie Chan, he would have more than likely noticed the gathering tsunami of global cinematic expansionism emanating from the California coastline, fueled by the rapidly changing technologies of mechanically-assisted animation, digital motion control, and optical compositing. Although far from determining his future course, each of these tendencies formed an important part of the context for the mutation in Hong Kong cinema in which Tsui Hark was about to play a central role, on the eve of the founding of his Film Workshop.

By the time Tsui Hark took the reins of *Zu: Warriors From the Magic Mountain* in Hong Kong, Hollywood was awash in special effects. The years from 1977 to 1983 were the gold rush years for George Lucas, Steven Spielberg, their imitators, and their progeny. Each new film, from the *Star Wars* cycle to *Close Encounters of the Third Kind, E.T., Superman, Alien, Blade Runner, Star Trek: The Motion Picture, Tron,* and *Raiders of the Lost Ark*, seemed to stretch the boundaries of technical innovation in visual effects design at speeds not seen since the boom years of the silent film industry in the US and Europe after World War I. A new type of dynamic moving image and highly plastic cinematic space seemed to be in formation and closely associated with proto-simulational optical technologies. Never mind that many of these films were equally effective in rolling narrative standards back toward the tastes of early adolescent white males: the threshold had been crossed. From this point on the modernist aesthetic and political experimentalism of Hollywood's own New Wave of the 1970s was relegated to the so-called "independent cinema" and to low-budget studio products. The commercial expectations of US film studios newly under diversified conglomerate ownership were, to a far greater degree, placed squarely on the shoulders of tech-savvy directors, special effects designers, and their ever-more elaborate works of immersive proto-simulation.[8]

Outside of Hollywood these sorts of films generally had an inhibiting industrial effect both in the short and the long terms. They raised economic barriers everywhere by increasing the costs of production, strongly influencing audience tastes and demands across national cultural markets for expensive production values, and drastically upping the scale of the standard marketing campaigns for individual films.[9] At the same time they successfully revisited Hollywood's classically cultural imperialist desire to market practically identical, tightly managed groups of films to larger and larger mass audiences on a world scale. In a world experiencing intensified forces of attraction toward rapidly evolving forms of financial and cultural integration, as Tsui Hark surely intimated, such a massive change in Hollywood's structures of dominance foretold a revised field of struggle for national film industries and independent filmmakers everywhere.

In the early 1980s Hong Kong's major film studios, many of them flush with cash and confidence from the rising value of Hong Kong's speculative financial markets during the territory's swift post-industrial transition, otherwise known as the inflation of a financially driven "bubble economy," were making their first truly aggressive efforts to invest in Hollywood since the heady days of Bruce Lee's *Enter the Dragon*.[10] We can tie this direct-investment tendency back to the predominant pastiche aesthetic in mainstream Hong Kong cinema, yet on a much higher scale of production values, optical technology and capital investment. In 1980, Run Run Shaw spent heavily on *Blade Runner,* Ridley Scott's landmark dystopian vision of a polyglot, post-human Los Angeles, and the first film to employ LucasFilm's Dykstraflex computer-aided motion control camera system on a recognizably terrestrial object — the city of Los Angeles — rather than the outer-space-bound industrial hulks of *2001*, *Star Wars* and *Alien*. Jackie Chan, and the organization built around him, thought the moment was ripe to bring his comedic kung-fu style to Hollywood, with decidedly mixed results, in the farcical action-comedy *Cannonball Run*. Not to be outdone, Golden Harvest, in particular the producer Leonard Ho, paid a record-setting sum, estimated at nearly HK$30 million, for Tsui Hark's production team to import visual effects designers from the US to consult on the local production of *Zu: Warriors From the Magic Mountain*. Whereas *Enter the Dragon* pioneered the co-produced star vehicle from Hollywood to Hong Kong, and *Blade Runner* returned the favor with investment capital from Hong Kong to Hollywood, *Zu: Warriors* made an audacious bet on the abilities of a regionally powerful but declining Hong Kong studio and a talented but wildly idiosyncratic young director to pull in top-shelf technical labor from Hollywood for the production of a local film to match the globe-straddling US giants.

In the short term, the bet was a failure. *Zu: Warriors From the Magic Mountain* was no blockbuster. It returned an estimated HK$3 million on its estimated HK$30million investment. Over time, as its reputation, audience and influence grew it made much of that money back. But without immediate ancillary marketing outlets or even a genuinely effective international distribution system beyond the region, it was an unrecoverable short-term loss. Tsui's solo crash raised fears industry-wide about their un-preparedness to confront head-on the new forces afoot in Hollywood. Partially as a result of the financial demise of *Zu: Warriors*, Hong Kong studios pulled back and did not rush to follow up on its technical, aesthetic, and industrial possibilities for nearly another decade. That job was left for Tsui Hark to do mainly on his own, as both producer and director. *Zu: Warriors From the Magic Mountain* was praised heavily by local film critics despite its losses, being nominated for Best Picture at that year's Third

Annual Hong Kong Film Awards. It was not, however, imitated by many others in the industry.[11]

With the spare exceptions of Tsui Hark's independently produced features, such as *A Chinese Ghost Story* and *Wicked City*, the marriage of Hong Kong action cinema with Hollywood's most advanced stages of special effects technology would not take place until sometime in the early-to-mid-1990s.[12] Even then, the union only grew in fits and starts, in many cases at a clear loss to the local industry through the export of Hong Kong's most elite strata of cultural producers, including Tsui himself, directly to Hollywood. By that reasoning, *Zu: Warriors* may appear to us now as an interesting but incomplete early footnote to the remarkable series of events taking place during the following decade. However, that interpretation fails to situate *Zu: Warriors* properly within the most important tendencies and technologies of its moment. Such a narrow interpretation adheres too strongly to an excessively confining theory of cultural change and historical influence, based upon direct temporal presences rather than the echoes of distant forbears. Although it was not an immediate cultural or economic breakthrough, *Zu: Warriors From the Magic Mountain* appears in retrospect to have been a foundational element of the source code for the technological and transnational transformation of Hong Kong cinema during the late-1980s and 1990s. In order to train ourselves to read that code we need to return to the film's technical composition in the context of the speculative frenzy of Hong Kong's 1980s bubble economy.

Mixed Economies of Optical Technologies

The assemblage of special effects designs on *Zu: Warriors* consisted of three distinct but interrelated networks: 1) Wire-work choreography, 2) conventional miniatures, make-up, pyrotechnics, and set design, and 3) optical compositing, rotoscoping, and matte painting, inspired largely by the success of Hollywood's special effects films from 1977 to 1983. Together, these factors produced a new type of hybrid cinematic space within Hong Kong action cinema, veering into the imminent creation of Hong Kong action as a new transnational popular style and a symptom of a new global spatial imagination. This new cinematic space was defined by corporeal fluidity, excessive speed, widely mobile and often 360-degree camera-work, virtual three-dimensionality, and constant visual mutation. The optical space produced by *Zu's* visual effects design was a space for the incessant transformation of substances, of the morphing of one form into another.

The fluid optical spaces of *Zu: Warriors* became doubly meaningful in terms of their intimate relation to a set of emergent, transnational cinematic production and technology networks. These networks can be effectively mapped in retrospect by using the people employed to consult on the film's composite images as our coordinate points. When we look at the resumes of the artists and designers imported by Tsui Hark to act as consultants and trainers (Robert Blalack, Peter Kuran, Arnie Wong, and John Scheele) we can start to make out the sinews of a web that Tsui imagined *Zu: Warriors* would be able to interface and help to re-weave.[13] It should be noted again clearly that Tsui brought these people to Hong Kong not to produce the film itself, but to act as advisors and consultants. In many cases their job was to advise poorly paid students in need of extensive training. This made for a number of costly fumbles on the set, as Tsui has recounted in recent interviews. "At that period of time, when we were trying to put together the sets, we had a problem because we had a group of students who were coming from school to work on our big effects. They stayed away for six months and came back with one or two shots. And I had found out one day — very shocking — they forgot to put the filter on the optical printer, so the film wasn't coming out the right color."[14] Utilizing the production-as-training tactic was perhaps ill advised in the short term, consequentially inflating the budget through the unexpected costs of their mistakes, but it fed directly into Tsui's innovative independent production strategies later in the decade at Film Workshop, which grew in part out of a student seminar at the University of Hong Kong. Many future effects producers in Hong Kong got their start in exactly this way. Nevertheless, by tracking these imported advisors we can make out much of the film's international technical horizon.

Robert Blalack began his career working for George Lucas on the original optical composites for *Star Wars*. That gave him a great deal of exposure to the new Dykstraflex motion control system that soon became the industry standard among optical compositors in Hollywood. Dykstraflex, named for its inventor, the American cinematographer John Dykstra, added computer controls and sophisticated database elements to complex camera movements in order to create exact duplicate electronic memories of those movements. This was essential to the work of optical compositing since the optical composite was such a demanding form in terms of the required labor inputs. Painstaking hour upon hour was spent re-photographing scenes for optical composite shots, since the optical composite demanded that a shot be taken over and over again using different visual elements each time. Each shot constituted a physical "layer," contained on a separate strip of celluloid that had to be run through an optical printer to re-photograph the image onto the previous visual layers. Without exact duplicate camera motions the slightest alteration or stutter could ruin the entire composite shot. As George Lucas was fond of saying, the special effects sequences for *Star Wars* would likely have been impossible in the absence of John Dykstra's on-the-spot invention.

In some ways, the informational and economic time lag preventing the widespread use of computer control systems in Hollywood prior to 1977 can explain much, but not all, of the limited deployment of these sorts of visual effects technologies between the release dates for *2001: A Space Odyssey* and *Star Wars*. It might also help to explain part, but not all, of their practically non-existent uptake in almost all other national film industries for a significantly longer time thereafter, especially in areas like Hong Kong. The amount of painstaking labor and the rising production costs on films demanding increasingly complex visual designs was one of the precipitating factors driving the use of three-dimensional computer graphics systems as automated replacements for mechanized optical tools. In any event, after their uptake into mainstream of US commercial filmmaking in the mid-1970s the scope of possible composite shots, and the numbers of available jobs in Hollywood related to the production of optical composites, began to widen with amazing speed. After *Star Wars,* Robert Blalack went on to experiment with optical composites for the sake of biomorphic representations in his early 1980s work on films such as *Wolfen* and Ken Russell's *Altered States*, helping to anticipate much of the subsequent digital work on the cinematic imaging of fluid, organic change of states.

Peter Kuran also got his start on the *Star Wars* films, working as an animation and rotoscope supervisor on *The Empire Strikes Back*. Rotoscoping was a form of mechanically assisted animation invented by Max Fleischer in 1917. It faded in and out of vogue for decades before gaining rapidly in use and currency among US special effects designers during the mid-to-late-1970s along with the increasing sophistication and ubiquity of optical compositing.[15] The rotoscope worked by mounting a combined camera and projector set-up on a translucent drawing table. Photographic images from the camera were projected onto the table so that an artist could trace them onto paper or animation cels, thereby transforming the photographic image into a drawn, animated image. The final traced images could then be used for the production of fully animated motion, such as Walt Disney's *Snow*

White from the 1930s or Ralph Bakshi's *Lord of the Rings* from the 1970s. They could also be used to combine hand-drawn animated images with photographic images through the use of an optical printer. In *Zu: Warriors From the Magic Mountain*, the swooping magical and electrical effects and colored overlays on the characters' swords were accomplished with the combined use of a rotoscope and an optical printer, much like the more spatially constrained light saber battles in *Star Wars*.

As with optical compositing in general, the key to rotoscoping was the creation of multiple layers of visual information, some photographic and some not, that could be coordinated in the printing process and recombined into moving images merging all of the layers into a coherent, post-photographic whole. In this way cinematographers and visual designers could "realistically" represent images that could not actually be photographed, either due to their prohibitive cost or to their physical impossibility. Partly due to its post-photographic nature, rotoscoping fed into various subsequent forms of digital imaging, either through the literal digitization of the process, recently realized on Richard Linklater's *Waking Life*, or the more common practice of integrating digitally animated and photographic effects into any number of "photorealistic" films such as *Jurassic Park* and *The Matrix*. Peter Kuran contributed much to the advancement of integrated photographic and digitally animated moving images later in his career with his work on films like *Toys* and *Men in Black*.

The other two visual effects designers imported by Tsui Hark to train local cultural workers for *Zu: Warriors*, Artie Wong and John Scheele, were not as accomplished as Blalack and Kuran. Nevertheless, they mapped out a significant portion of the technological map of the film's eventual aims and actual production. Wong and Scheele worked on the making of Disney's *Tron*, the first commercial narrative film to feature three-dimensional computer graphics as significant elements of the story. Wong worked as a matte painter while Scheele was a technical supervisor more directly connected to composing *Tron*'s digital and optical elements. Matte painting, like rotoscoping, was an older technology whose significance grew by leaps and bounds during the late-70s special-effects gold rush. Mattes were background images, often painted on large sheets of glass to allow light to penetrate and achieve a sense of visual depth-of-field, forming a crucial layer of information in the optical composite. Mattes have now been fully integrated into the digital production of background and landscape elements. Hand-painted elements now rarely appear in commercial cinema. While the pioneering use of 3-D computer graphics in narrative commercial cinema was also clearly *Tron*'s most significant outcome, playing a role in Tsui's own decisions later in the decade to pursue digital animation through Cinefex Workshop, there is little question that its optical composites were equally expert and labor-intensive, and perhaps equally influential in Tsui's decision to employ two of its designers as consultants.

As we trace the contours of this technical map, revealing multiple avenues into the age of simulated and digitized moving images, it is important to recognize that the images being sold by Hollywood and bought by Hong Kong as the most advanced of their moment, the ones that pushed hardest inside the industry towards the literal identification of the moving image with synthetic optical technologies, were actually unevenly developed assemblages of diverse technologies. Each element of these technological assemblages emerged for distinct ends and at multiple speeds. In many cases, the most successful were really only moderately updated assemblages of much older optical technologies that had fallen out of favor in dominant industry paradigms during the studio upheaval of the 1940s, 1950s, and 1960s. This was true even in the case of the Dykstraflex system, which at the most basic level simply added a computer control system, a thin layer of digital information, on top of pre-existing Panaflex cameras.

Special effects in the 1970s and early 1980s were the products of *mixed technological economies* spanning time periods, territories, and technologies. These mixed economies fed directly into short-term demands throughout the advanced capitalist world for movies featuring optical composites, as well as long-term demands for the full-scale digital automation of the compositing process. The reasons for this are many. It is notable, for instance, that the optical composite was such a labor-intensive and often hand-made craft, produced under diverse conditions and often widely separated times and spaces, in many cases despite the existence of effective communications networks. When the first serious wave of digital production hit, many of the pioneers of optical compositing were immediately thrown out of work. Later, their compatriots in the old-fashioned model-building and matte-painting units would suffer the same fate unless they retrained themselves for the age of digitization. At the same time, Michelle Pierson's dissection of US special effects fan discourse indicates that optically composited images often showed their seams, or the traces of the composition, and that those seams were widely noted and discussed throughout fan literatures.[16] That sort of audience discourse tended, as much as the intensive application of industrial discipline to cultural workers, toward a desire within Hollywood for technologies that would erase the perception of distinction among coordinated fragments. The tendency toward the erasure of origins fostered by the rise of digital compositing was fantasized but not yet realized by the effects wave of the late-1970s and early-1980s, regardless of national context.

Based on an understanding of the uneven development of optical technologies it should not surprise anyone that optical compositing also unevenly fostered new forms of technical and cultural coordination at the point of production in order to manage diverse relationships between cultural fragments and optical technologies. Its uses fostered an intensified logic of filmmaking as the exertion of technical control over widely dispersed visual fragments. There is little question that *Zu: Warriors* played into that concept of filmmaking as control mechanism, or the production of imaginary visual coherence out of real fragmentation. Yet had *Zu: Warriors* merely turned toward the application of optical compositing and rotoscope technologies to compose its cinematic spaces and motions, it would merely have reproduced the mixed economy already popularized by Hollywood. It did not do this. Instead, *Zu: Warriors* effectively re-contextualized those technologies into a new type of virtually three-dimensional and extremely mobile, fluid cinematic space by linking Hollywood's networks to local technological networks already marginalized to an even greater degree by Hollywood.

The film's remarkable imagery, and much of its eventual influence, was the result of an unusual collision between state-of-the-art optical effects design and the distinctively Hong Kong cinematic tradition of wire-work martial arts choreography. Yuen Biao (Bruce Lee's double in the bizarre, posthumous *Game of Death*), Hoi Mang, Hark-On Fang, and Cory Yuen were all exceptionally talented young fight choreographers from the Cantonese stage tradition, who played significant roles in their own ways in pushing the martial arts cinema past the bodily authenticity of Bruce Lee towards Tsui Hark's cinema of boundless speed and super-human fantasy. *Zu: Warriors* was thus a complex assemblage of aesthetics, spatial practices, and optical technologies that remains difficult to classify outside the language of transnational networks, evaporating boundaries and uneven developments. The film's distinctive sense of movement and cinematic space was a result of that mostly untried assemblage, performed experimentally in a pressure-cooker commercial environment.

In the most cliché sense, one might break that assemblage into an East-meets-West dichotomy, with Cantonese operatic set construction, miniatures, pyrotechnics, and traditional wire-based martial stage choreography jostling with the latest imports from L.A. The obvious trouble with such a breakdown is that it depends upon a linked dichotomy between tradition and modernity, reproduced in the colonial paradigm, with local elements struggling to absorb the "modern" Western elements into the meshwork of mythic narrative. *Zu: Warriors From the Magic Mountain* might appear to be the localization, pure and simple, of optical compositing. However, that description should be obviously unsatisfying, and not only for its racially coded colonialist and Orientalist overtones. On the one hand, it dislocates wire-work stage choreography from the history of the Hong Kong cinema's struggle throughout the 1970s to discover a new international identity and a new cinematic style in the aftermath of Bruce Lee's untimely death, covering the technique's actually contested standing within the industry, in competition with Lee's aesthetic of corporeal authenticity, with a wet blanket of stereotypical traditionalism.

On the other hand, and perhaps much more seriously, the East-West binary fails to address the ways that the hybrid spaces of *Zu: Warriors* were actually retrieved by Hollywood's own visual and spatial imaginations at a subsequent moment, taking their place eventually at the core of the dominant global image apparatus. Tsui Hark's images were in that sense *prefigurative*, not merely resistant. Rather than mere localization, we can detect a new stage in the transnational production of popular culture. Given the ways that *Zu*'s technical assemblages served as early prototypes for the changes in cinematic styles and visual designs in Hong Kong and Hollywood, not to mention French, British, Japanese, and Indian, action films of the late-1990s, we might say that Hollywood's architects of optical technologies and finance capital did not catch up with *Zu: Warriors* for nearly two decades. The cultural and technological assemblage posed by *Zu: Warriors* was ultimately experienced as a long-term crisis within Hollywood, though one not immediately acknowledged until the rise of photo-realistic digital effects technologies. At that point however, the liquid forces of cultural, technological, and financial globalization had already penetrated deeply into Hollywood's core imaginary.

Boundless Fluidity

> A *space* exists when one takes into consideration (along with location or position) vectors of direction, velocities, and time variables. Thus space is composed of intersections of mobile elements. It is in a sense actuated by the ensemble of movements deployed within it.
> — Michel De Certeau, *The Practice of Everyday Life*[17]

The production of cinematic space in *Zu: Warriors* took shape within the fiscal context of the film's material production. Financial factors played a key role in leading Tsui toward the realization of his extremely plastic and highly mobile spatial visions. These factors lay mainly in the rising confidence of Hong Kong film producers during the bubble economy of the 1970s and 1980s. Financial speculation and the globalization of markets produced an emergent consumer middle-class in Hong Kong seeking a balance between local and cosmopolitan identities. Yet such an imaginary space in between locality and cosmopolitanism was perpetually elusive. As Ackbar Abbas points out, expanding on Paul Virilio's ideas, the emergent space of the new post-industrial Hong Kong is a space of "disappearance," or the incessant mutation of material global flows such that the existent built space is always already in the process of becoming other. *Zu: Warriors* was a prime example of that process, emerging straight from the crucible of the early-1980s finance capitalism to become momentarily the most expensive film ever financed by a Hong Kong studio at the same time that it ranked among its worst failures. *Zu: Warriors* signified in the very same text both the inflation and the bursting of Hong Kong's speculative financial bubble.

Linkage between the desires of finance capital and the commercial fortunes of advanced visual technologies follows the path blazed by globalizing Hollywood itself. At some level the conclusion is unavoidable that *Zu* was just as guilty of "putting the money on the screen" — of literally taking as its task the visualizing of the desires of finance capital — as just about any other effects-driven blockbuster. In fact, the trailer for the film's Hong Kong release featured images of a press conference treating not only the technological images but also *the consultants themselves* as featured elements of the studio's investment. This problem contains added folds and dimensions related not only to *Zu*'s mytho-political allegories or to its eventual commercial fortunes, but to the transformation of finance capital itself from an instrument of investment and production to an increasingly weightless form based on the alchemy of pure exchange value in the age of self-referential financial instruments like the junk bond and the derivative. Changes in the nature of finance capital were reflected in the changing climate for film production and distribution. They were in turn re-signified by the cinematic visualization of a new kind of fluid, imaginary space for action of the sort that increasingly marked the popular imaginary space of digital morphology and real-time global markets for the next two decades.

In other words, Tsui Hark's and Golden Harvest's interests in imported optical effects technologies turned at least in part on the commercial potential of the newly dominant global optical technologies. That observation should lead one to expect that significant aspects of that commercial motivation would be signified and realized in the uses of the technologies themselves. *Zu: Warriors'* hybrid spatial morphology registered significant aspects of its commercial interests, but with ultimately incomplete techniques dependent upon re-using or even misusing an assemblage of machines, which themselves were derived from earlier modes of cultural production. The film stood at a transitional moment and bore the competing traces of unevenly developing historical tendencies. Yet, it remains to be seen exactly how those tendencies manifested during the production of *Zu: Warriors'* hybrid visual spaces and its selective tactics of postmodern pastiche. Understood perhaps in Henri Lefebvre's terms, as a "representational overlay" on the spatial practices of Hong Kong's post-industrial social field, potentially constituting a structured array of actions in between colonialism and globalism, what sorts of actions might the spaces of *Zu: Warriors* have either produced or foreclosed?[18]

Perhaps the best examples of the film's distinctive spatial composition were the film's "morphs." Ordinarily, the "morph" is identified almost exclusively with the rise of three-dimensional digital imagery such as the liquid metal antagonist of *Terminator 2*. Images of change in organic states have of course preoccupied world cinema at least since the rise of montage aesthetics, first in the Soviet Union and then Hollywood in the 1920s, but not until the rise of digital compositing and control systems was each state of a visual sequence able to be fully and fluidly merged with each other state, effectively erasing the signs of fragmentation into an illusory perception of continuity. Optical compositing ought perhaps to be seen as an incomplete mid-way point between layered montage and digital compositing. Certain optically composited body morphs, like the ones found in *Zu: Warriors From the Magic Mountain*, prefigured the eventual look of the digital morph even though these images remained attached to the staggered fluidity of the montage. Much of that incompleteness was compensated for by even older techniques of high-speed editing. Tsui Hark's lighting quick cuts looked forward to a popular cinema of shortened attention spans and the pure aesthetic enjoyment of speed, as much as they looked backward to the origins of visual effects in discoveries made by early twentieth century filmmakers like Georges Melies that startling visual transformations could be effected using little more than the capacity of the camera itself to juxtapose image sequences in non-linear order.[19] In the morphs of *Zu: Warriors* we can therefore detect part of the meaning and purpose of Tsui Hark's signature style, his extremely high-speed, almost vertiginous editing. Many of the most remarkable "morph" images in *Zu: Warriors* were in fact composed via the old-fashioned editing table at least as much as by the rotoscope table.

Take, for instance, the scene where the Blood Demon's double, in the guise of Ting Yin, confronts Ti Ming-chi and Yi Chen, who have just caught a fish. The sequence begins with a closeup shot from behind Ting Yin's head as a glowing deep red band creeps up the tassel of his headpiece. This is a rotoscope shot that adds a hand-drawn visual layer on top of the photographic shot. The next shot is a medium of Ting Yin with legs apart, elaborately posing and reaching just behind his head to send a bolt of energy down to the characters below. The shot reverses to Ti Ming-chi and Yi Chen as Ti Ming-chi vaults onto Yi Chen's shoulder to avoid the flying bolt of energy, still hand-drawn, that arrives from the upper left-hand corner of the screen and plummets to the lower right. This too is a rotoscope shot that cuts a precise geometric angle across the field of action, establishing an almost impossibly fluid three-dimensional space within the two-dimensional frame. The movement of the bolt is echoed by Ti Ming-chi's graceful flip onto Yi Chen's shoulder as the bolt returns looping around from behind and blasting out directly toward the camera. Seemingly from nowhere, another bolt swoops over the two students and back over their heads, again directly toward the camera. Ting Yin's sword has been transformed into an image of pure energy, allowing it to attack quickly at a distance. Over a couple of very fast-paced seconds, the space of on-screen action is taken over exclusively by the interactions between rotoscoped images, in coordination with

Fig. 3.1 Stage 1: The swordsman's body is overlaid with an optical rotoscope, signifying its impending transformation

Fig. 3.2 Stage 2: The swordsman's body disappears into shower of color

Fig. 3.3   Stage 3: The swordsman's body is transmitted across space through the image of a solid red wave

Fig. 3.4   Stage 4: The swordsman's body is re-constituted, this time as the female body of the Countess

the more modest and restrained actions of the human characters. When the real Ting Yin then appears to challenge the Blood Demon, his double morphs into a doubled image of the Countess in brilliant red robes.

Examining these shots frame-by frame reveals an exaggerated pose by Ting Yin's double signifying the will to transform his body, and then a series of colorful rotoscoped overlays onto this image. A force seems to emerge from within the center of his person, signified as a spattering bubble of colors. These emerging layers shift into a more conventional blue outline, coupled to another speeding color burst, before finally exploding outward like the flame of a Roman candle. The shot immediately cuts from that delirious spray of light into a single thick red wave oscillating through the air towards a rocky outcropping. The superimposed red wave is substituted by the Countess's flowing red robes via an extremely fast cut between the rotoscoped frame and the frame containing the photographic image of a piece of red cloth in motion. The edit itself effects the mutation, yet the edit would not have been possible without the sharp juxtaposition between the immaterial rotoscoped image and the material shot of the waving cloth. An image of material substance has thus been dematerialized and re-materialized in and through staccato pattern of visual substitutions. From that pattern, itself clearly staggered into perceptibly discrete moments, emerges the perception of a fluid, virtually three-dimensional cinematic space. The idea of this space was not the outcome of any particular technology but was literally composed by the carefully orchestrated series of rotoscoped overlays on top of photographic images of Ting Yin's exaggeratedly mobile body, coupled to quick edits between the images. That the apparent content of the sequence indicates the transmogrification of male into female, treating the self itself as a sort of fluid substance to be passed back and forth between contingent states of being, only enhances the significance of the sequence. The space of visual fluidity across photographic boundaries is then also a space of fluid interchange between the gendered boundaries of the self. Nevertheless, the overlaid non-photographic visual information always fails to resolve into the photographic. We can tell fairly easily where the one layer ends and the other begins, even if the transition is merely a split-second jump.

Likewise, consider the sequence where the Countess "freezes" Ting Yin, Ti Ming-chi and Yi Chen. This sequence of shots begins from on high, watching the Countess swoop into the central chamber, arms outstretched before her. An optically printed overlay reveals a tangle of hot blue lines emanating from her palms and fingertips, directly in line with the forward motion of her body, pointing down toward the body of Ting Yin. The next frame sharply cuts to an overhead shot of a life-sized figure of Ting Yin wrapped in a coating of opaque plastic, plummeting to the floor below. The Countess spreads her arms and the continuous downward motion of the falling figure inserts the immobilized body into a line of visual continuity with the initial rotoscoped overlay. Wire-work animates the flying body of the Countess, making her steep angle of descent across the frame possible and expanding the visual axis of the shot across three dimensions. Quick editing between rotoscoped and photographic images creates an imperfect illusion of Ting Yin's physical mutation. Each sequence remains functionally dependent on the others despite the discordance in their production, wrapping the entire assemblage into the hybrid logic of cinematic space as a field for the material transformation of physical spaces (including the body itself) into spaces for the realistic transcendence of the boundaries and limitations of the physical world.

Zu's cinematic spaces of constant mutation and the transcendence of physical limits reach their apotheosis in the sequence leading to the final confrontation between Ting Yin, Ti Ming-chi, and Yi Chen. When Ti Ming-chi and Yi Chen reach Lady Li I-chi their physical landscape shifts in between their mountaintop perch and an abstract miasma of pure light and color. The abstract backgrounds were produced using a relatively standard blue-screen superimposition. When combined with their elegant wire-worked flying motions, however, these background seem deliriously lightweight and mobile, as if the rules of the physical world have been left behind, in favor of an altogether imaginary set of laws. Those alternate physical laws find their realization in the ideal of instantaneous communications, or the joining of minds into unison that will enable the linkage of the Twin Swords. The mystical overlay of this idea parallels the imaginary desires of future development in the composition of a "real" space composed purely of communication itself, or the utopian imaginary space of the emergent information society wherein Hong Kong serves as the conduit for cultures and data rather than a space for the materialization of physical goods production.

This folding of space into bizarre new domains of instantaneous and perfectly realized communications, pictured literally by split screens and the substitution of audio tracks to simulate the merger of minds and voices across time and space, raises both fears and desires for the characters and the audience. As many critics have argued, this sort of imagery embodies and in a sense prefigures the imagination of the digital sublime, wherein information exchange supplants the physical world with a perfect reproduction, minus the frictions of non-virtual space, including subjective identity itself. When Ti Ming-chi and Yi Chen begin to speak with the voice of Lady Li I-chi they look to one another and anxiously ask, "Are we still men?" To this she replies, "Of course, you have no need to worry," although it is clear for all to see that the ideal of universal subjective unification contains within it the distinct possibility of rapidly evaporating boundaries between and within selves that have already been reconfigured according to an instantaneous informational model. They may still be "men," yet the ultimate success of their quest will transform their fixed identities into provisional constructs, or momentary accumulations of force in perpetually shifting positional wars. On this possibility rests the social imagination of the film.

Rushing to return to the real world in order to prevent the final eruption of the Blood Demon and its forces of fragmentation into human history, Ti Ming-chi and Yi Chen are forced to confront Ting Yin, who interposes himself and acts as a literal boundary between the Twin Swords. All three float in a miasmic space of pure color and abstraction that is only traversed by instantaneous communications. This space is entirely opaque to them except through the navigational powers of high-speed logistical coordination, which allows Ti Ming-chi and Yi Chen to find one another in the fog and stay on track toward the final unification of minds. Their effort only succeeds, however, through the sacrificial act of the Countess, casting herself at Ting Yin and propelling them both outside the space of the film's narrative resolution. Her act articulates an instantaneous ethic of unity beyond the merely technical aspects of the film's high-speed communicational

Yi Chen, what kind of witchcraft is this?

Fig. 3.5 Ti Ming-chi and Yi Chen float in the disorienting, fluid space of their final confrontation with the Blood Demon

imagination, yet nevertheless visualized in and through the mutable visual space of the film's hybrid technical assemblage. In effect, the Countess's sacrifice completes the ethic of boundless virtual space and contingent selfhood by calling for a new regulatory ideal of transcendent unity wherein the authentic self is sacrificed not for any particular power but for the sake of the supra-national ideals of "love" and "perpetual peace." In that idea, and in the miasmic and polymorphic space of the film itself, lay Tsui Hark's conception of transnational cultural production.

If we can say that *Zu: Warriors From the Magic Mountain* exemplifies the triumph of a postmodern pastiche aesthetic in Hong Kong cinema by systematically borrowing and remaking the decontextualized fragments of Hollywood's hardware and software, then we must also say that it looks beyond the fragmentary domain of the global postmodern towards a new form of interconnected transnational culture premised upon a thoroughly technological optics along with a speed of communications and cultural flow tending towards what Paul Virilio has described as the virtual state of "real time."[20] More to the point, while recognizing both tendencies we still need to understand the significance of their interconnection within the film as a whole. At the heart of *Zu: Warriors* lay a dialectical composite of fragmentation and unification that echoes throughout its technical and narrative compositions. Although *Zu: Warriors* begins and ends in a mythically fragmented China it overlays the notion that the future lies beyond any territory whatsoever. The characters must come back down to earth, yet only to leap in the air once more. At no point does the composite ever fully resolve into one side or the other. Yet, the nature of its material position within the technical networks most responsible for globalizing the optical composite led its form of transnational culture increasingly towards the identification with the forces of globalization itself. That this would happen was perhaps predictable, but it was not forseen at the time.

Whereas the mixed technological economies of the early-1980s still allowed space for imperfection and incompleteness in the technologized moving image, its imaginary space of instantaneous communications, aesthetic fluidity, and physical mutability arced towards the evasion of territory and the loss of the residual materiality of the self during Hong Kong cinema's rapid digitization and financial deterritorialization in the 1990s.

The question which announced itself with ringing clarity in the years between *Zu: Warriors From the Magic Mountain* and the making of its digital successor, *Legend of Zu*, in the late-1990s, was whether or not Tsui's visionary visuality might be swallowed up after all — not by the enormity of Chinese territorial nationalism but by the light speed forms of transnational aesthetics and globalized cultural production. Tsui Hark has remained self-conscious over time about that possibility, perhaps to the point of accelerating his own visual aesthetic beyond the point of any easy acceptance in the global popular mainstream. Many have argued that even in the age of music videos and hyperventilating TV commercials the speed of Tsui Hark's editing and storytelling inhibits the possibility of his worldwide commercial acceptance. To what degree he cares about this matter ultimately only Tsui Hark can answer. History, however, does not generally move in conscious directions or precise patterns. The forces that most threaten the stability and coherence of Tsui's anticipatory vision are also the forces that prompted the creation of *Zu: Warriors* in the first place. *Zu: Warriors From the Magic Mountain* helped perhaps in small but significant ways to advance them.

4

Technologies of Transnationalism:
Digitization, Globalization, and the Long March Toward *Legend of Zu*

> The contemporary systems of communication are not
> subordinated to sovereignty; on the contrary, sovereignty seems
> to be subordinated to communication — or actually, sovereignty
> is articulated through communications systems. In the field of
> communication, the paradoxes that bring about the dissolution
> of territorial and/or national sovereignty are more clear than ever.
>   - Michael Hardt and Antonio Negri, *Empire*[1]

After *Zu: Warriors From the Magic Mountain* was released in the
Asian market, Golden Harvest made plans to release a North
American version as well. For some reason, maybe imagining that
a period drama on Chinese mythology would never sell in the North
American market of 1983, they decided that the version of the film
sold in Asia would fail to find a significant audience. To solve this
anticipated problem, producers at Golden Harvest demanded that
Tsui Hark add a few extra minutes at the beginning and at the end
of the film as modern "bookends" to the plot. These "bookends,"

they thought, would help to translate *Zu* to non-Chinese audiences, bringing it closer into line with trends in Hong Kong cinema towards contemporary urban settings. In the new sections, Yuen Biao's character became an ordinary person living in present day Hong Kong who experienced a knock on the head that plunged him into the otherwise unaltered film world of *Zu: Warriors From the Magic Mountain*. In the end, he woke up and realized that he'd been dreaming the entire time, thus explaining away the tropes of *wuxia* as being nothing more than the empty signs of a hallucinatory dreamworld. Titled *Zu: Time Warriors*, its release was an even worse commercial fiasco than *Zu: Warriors* itself. Needless to say, the additions were hardly improvements. North American audiences still found the plot difficult to follow, neither being used to the speed of Tsui's storytelling nor the tropes of *wuxia*. Tsui was angered by the producers' intrusions. He vowed to bury the film and never to work with a conventional Hong Kong studio again. *Zu: Time Warriors* remains an almost impossible object to track down today, except in degraded bootleg copies.[2] Nevertheless, the events surrounding its creation proved to be decisive in turning Tsui Hark toward the choices that made him perhaps the most influential Hong Kong filmmaker of his time.

Nearly two decades passed before Tsui revisited the mythological world of *Zu*. One might claim that films like *A Chinese Ghost Story* and *A Chinese Ghost Story II* continued in their own ways the worldview, the narrative ambience and the engagement with *wuxia* that Tsui initiated on *Zu: Warriors From the Magic Mountain*. However, these films were both produced and advertised as their own distinctive projects. *Legend of Zu*, produced in the fateful year of 1999, arguably the low point financially for the Hong Kong film industry as a whole, was another matter. This time Tsui returned explicitly to the mythos of *Zu: Warriors From the Magic Mountain,* but on very different economic and industrial terms. Tsui was far more in control of the production process on *Legend of Zu*. He was able to stamp his ideas on the film directly without interference from studio bosses. Yet, Hong Kong cinema was in a state of virtual commercial free-fall. At times it seemed that almost every company was hemorrhaging money. Top stars were fleeing for greener pastures in the US and Europe. Digital technology had almost entirely replaced the older optical forms, seeming to allow a more precise visualization of Tsui's elaborate full-motion imagination. Yet, the new practices of digital imaging and compositing carried with them additional financial, political and aesthetic risks. Tsui has seemed in recent interviews to be well aware of these risks. Digital technologies, linking diverse genres, corporations, and cultural production processes into ever-tighter webs of continuous flow and exchange, threatened to subsume the autonomy of the Hong Kong action cinema within the uncertain new geographies of a deracinated, transnational media culture.

The Fallout From *Zu*: Building Film Workshop and Cinefex

During the years in between the production and release dates for *Zu: Warriors From the Magic Mountain* and *Legend of Zu*, Tsui Hark made over a dozen feature films, all of them either produced or directed under the banner of his own company, Film Workshop. Born from the ashes of his experience with Golden Harvest, the founding of Film Workshop in 1984 marked the beginning of a fertile collaboration between Tsui Hark and his wife, the producer Nansun Shi, then working for Cinema City.[3] They were tired of feeling that successful filmmakers needed to make constant trade-offs between artistry and commerce and wanted to create a place where they could initiate work with the ability to slip between the cracks of the industry's restrictive genre and production categories.

They also wanted to make complex and meaningful films that still made money. Film Workshop had strong ties not only to the common organizational forms of independent productions houses all over the world, but also to international traditions of "auteur" filmmaking which sought to raise standards in the commercial cinema by empowering talented film directors to stamp their "personal" visions on celluloid.[4] As they describe it today in their promotional materials, the original dream of Film Workshop was "to create a workshop where the foremost filmmakers could work on films with artistic merit, and at the same time commercially rewarding for the financiers" (sic).[5] Amazingly enough, given the intensity of the competition and the notorious infidelity of popular audiences, their idea seems to have paid off.

The continuing health and vitality of Film Workshop over the past two decades was secured mainly by a string of smash commercial hits produced immediately following the initial formation of the company. *Shanghai Blues*, which Tsui Hark has described as his personal favorite among all of his films, was only a moderate hit in absolute box office numbers, but it successfully reversed the disastrous cost-to-income ratio of *Zu: Warriors From the Magic Mountain*. Having been made for less than HK$4 million, it took in just under HK$12 million, and this time for a company in which Tsui was the principle stakeholder, not merely a hired hand. *A Better Tomorrow*, which launched the careers of its director, John Woo, and co-star, Chow Yun-fat, on their well known trajectories toward international superstardom, was a runaway blockbuster in Hong Kong, taking in just over HK$34 million and being voted Best Picture at the 1987 Hong Kong Film Awards. *A Better Tomorrow* also initiated a lucrative string of sequels, a trend that Film Workshop repeated over the next decade with the *Once Upon a Time in China, A Chinese Ghost Story,* and *Swordsman* series. *Peking Opera Blues* was equally well lauded at the 1987 Hong Kong Film Awards while taking in just over HK$17 million at the box office. On the strength of those three profitable films, Film Workshop was suddenly in a position to expand its operations and to begin investing heavily in the visual effects technologies that had made *Zu: Warriors From the Magic Mountain* possible, long before other filmmakers or studios in Hong Kong even considered such a move.

Film Workshop had great financial and critical success in 1986, and the same year also saw the founding of Cinefex Workshop, the special effects arm of the company. In many ways, it was Cinefex Workshop, not the "auteurist" standards of independence, which made Film Workshop different from any other production company formed in Hong Kong during the 1980s. At the outset, Cinefex Workshop was divided into four interrelated sub-units. The Optical Unit handled optical printing, rotoscoping, cel animation, masking, and matte painting. The Physical Unit handled mechanical effects, pneumatic effects, pyrotechnics, miniatures, puppets, prosthetics, models, and make-up. The Production Unit handled storyboards, miniature cinematography, stop-motion animation, and claymation. The Computer Unit took over digital graphics production, motion control, and digital compositing. Although initially the least significant of the organization's units, seeing the least amount of work, within five years the Computer Unit had absorbed the vast majority of new investment and kept Cinefex Workshop at least loosely in-step with the early 1990s boom in 3-D computer graphics and digital compositing that were fueling Hollywood's ever-more expensive, globally dominant blockbuster films.

The obvious prototype for the organization of Cinefex Workshop, although it was never really stated as such, was Lucasfilm's spinoff corporation, Industrial Light and Magic (ILM).[6] Following the tremendous box office and merchandising successes of the first *Star Wars* film, George Lucas blazed a trail later followed by Tsui Hark by turning his effects production unit for that film into its own semi-autonomous corporate entity. This had numerous long-term benefits, although few in Hollywood foresaw them at the time. First, he could lower the cost of production on special effects for his own films by keeping production costs in-house. Second, he could contract out his facilities and crews for production work on other film and TV projects, thereby generating revenue even when not in production on Lucasfilm features. Finally, perhaps following the inspiration of the Dykstraflex invention, he could sponsor research and development in special effects, thereby generating revenue on the technologies themselves, not merely on film production and sales. Lucas followed this route in the coming years by investing in sound reproduction, and even moving into theatrical exhibition technologies. Many corporations in Hollywood later followed the ILM model, fostering a fast-growing cluster of effects houses around Los Angeles. Yet, without massive infusions of start-up capital, of the sort provided by Lucas' films and ILM's early lead in effects production, smaller companies were at a consistent competitive disadvantage. They became "boutique" shops. Film Workshop was no exception, although it has operated for most of its existence in a drastically different competitive environment than most US effects houses by being almost entirely regional, and thus not in the running for production contracts for companies and crews based in California. The visual effects business in the 1980s, while pushing forward in some ways the incessant globalization of Hollywood's business structures, had itself not yet expanded and interconnected globally. At least it had not done so in the manner achieved by the end of the 1990s with the rush to "offshore" effects production by US companies seeking lower costs, towards Australia, New Zealand, South Korea, and, slowly but surely, mainland China.[7]

Part of the initial desire for Cinefex Workshop was not simply to support Tsui's continued personal work, but to modernize the production values of Hong Kong cinema as such by taking the local lead in special effects production. This turned out to be a longer-term project than anticipated. Cinefex learned much from the expensive and often frustrating experience of importing design labor from the US for *Zu: Warriors From the Magic Mo*untain. It sought to control costs and to increase their proportion of the effects market by encouraging Hong Kong filmmakers to use their facilities. To a certain degree, one can understand films like *A Chinese Ghost Story* and *Wicked City* as local showcases for the talents of Cinefex Workshop. Other companies were not so quick to follow suit. Even if they could not compete head-on with Hollywood though, then they could at least encourage a facsimile of Hollywood's emerging effects houses in Hong Kong. There were both advantages and disadvantages to this idea. If any problem stood out above the rest, it was that Cinefex never really had sufficient capital for research and development. This meant that they were in a position of perpetual dependency on networks comprised of US, European, and Japanese hardware and software companies in order to keep up with new developments in digital animation and compositing.

In 1991 they made their first major push into the digital realm by importing significant numbers of high-end workstations from Silicon Graphics, the groundbreaking graphical hardware company founded in 1982 by Jim Clarke, later the CEO of Netscape. Silicon Graphics had by that time become the industry standard in commercial computer graphics and digital compositing by veering away from general-use computing, in favor of workstations specifically designated for the arduous number crunching involved in 3-D graphics production. The advantage of this sort of integrated hardware from a purely pragmatic point of view was that it enabled the automation of most of the compositing and design process by building rendering and post-production effects directly into the overall framework of the hardware. For instance, the so-called "geometry engine" transferred most algorithmic calculations for geometrical wire-frame modeling straight onto the processor. That meant that an artist could directly manipulate a 3-D object in real time without making the computer waste time reading through thousands of lines of code. Designating processor functions in this way sped up the entire graphical production process and fundamentally changed the relations between silicon and celluloid technologies, but it also made the systems extremely expensive and difficult to adapt over time. Early users of Silicon Graphics systems mostly included high-end Hollywood production teams, along with US military and space program simulators, corporate industrial designers, and high-end university and private laboratory-based scientific researchers. Perceptions that these sorts of networks were sprouting from the soil of the Silicon Graphics workstation, among similar technologies, led many observers to begin describing the existence of a "military-entertainment-industrial complex" which appeared to be directing a growing and disproportionate share of the world economy towards the United States.

Whether or not one describes the form of global economic integration and expansion witnessed in the 1990s as being singularly unequal and unfairly tilted towards the United States and its corporate emissaries, there is little doubt that Film Workshop and Cinefex quickly saw their interests diverging with the workstation mode of production and converging with tendencies toward smaller and cheaper forms of hardware and software. They resisted head-on competition with Hollywood, preferring to focus instead on Tsui's own films and regional Asian media contracts. At the same time that Steven Spielberg's first installment in his *Jurassic Park* series, powered by Silicon Graphics 3-D rendering hardware, was becoming the first Hollywood film to hit number one at the Hong Kong box office, Cinefex began searching for ways to defray the massive initial cost of its technology purchases while remaining a vital source of digital post-production in an industry largely resistant to large-scale technological investment and regularization of production methods. Although the Hong Kong film industry had not yet hit the hard times of the late-1990s, conditions were beginning to sour.

In the mid-1990s Cinefex moved gradually away from reliance on designated workstation systems, towards cheaper software-based systems like FLINT, designed and produced by Discreet Logic, Inc. A forerunner and continuing competitor to contemporary programs like Maya, by Alias|Wavefront, FLINT deployed cheaper off-the-shelf hardware components, at a later stage in desktop PC development, and returned many of the formerly integrated graphic al calculating functions to software and graphics cards. While lowering costs, it also enabled higher-profits in contracts with Asian production companies and furthered the rationalization of the famously irregular Hong Kong film production process. As one Cinefex worker described it in 1995, "By bringing in digital tools like FLINT, our capabilities for producing impressive effects increased enormously. It changed the way directors are working. The notorious haphazard methods are giving way to a more thoroughly thought-out approach to filming, involving effects animators at the pre-production phase."[8] Time-consuming optically printed effects were almost completely eliminated as digital post-production was tightly integrated into the overall workflow.

Following the lead of Film Workshop and Cinefex, Hong Kong cinema moved in fits and starts towards a full-scale rationalization of its production methods and integration with transnational networks of high-tech media production during its digital phase of development.[9] This change is still incomplete, in part because it contrasts so sharply with long-held beliefs and practices concerning the basic value of personalism over institutionalism in Hong Kong's cultural production.[10] Mixed economies of culture and technology have persisted in the face of pressures for global integration, in part for pragmatic reasons related to the ongoing difficulties of "photorealistic" animation. In parallel with efforts to raise money for film production from transnational financial networks, digital production hooked Hong Kong cinema into wider webs of technological investment and cinematic style than had been possible during the making of the first *Zu: Warriors*. Virtually everyone could now use the same machines and many of the same methods. Yet, the local industry as a whole remained unsure about how best to respond to a newly aggressive, globally oriented Hollywood. There was no single best answer. Ancillary revenue streams have been slow to evolve, while low-grade digital piracy has undercut the profitability of the industry as a whole. Even so, pictures of a revived relation of core and periphery, derived from the cultural imperialist theory, are misleading. Culture and technology persistently flow in more than one direction.

Instead of a cut-and-dried re-run of past imperialisms, something distinctly new has seemed to be happening to each industry's most popular and profitable films. Hong Kong cinema took up residency in the core of the dominant global image apparatus at the exact moment that the local industry threatened to go belly up. During this time the two industries began sharing larger and larger areas of overlap in the production process, including shared technologies and methods. Later, they started to overlap in terms of narrative form, style and in personnel. While John Woo was off making his first successful forays into mainstream Hollywood production, detaching himself more and more over time from his connections to the local industry, Tsui Hark was busy funneling his incomes from a pair of mediocre Jean-Claude Van Damme thrillers back into the coffers of Film Workshop, in preparation for his remarkable digital animations of the late-1990s, including integrated 2-D cels and 3-D graphics on *A Chinese Ghost Story (The Tsui Hark Animation)* and *Master Q 2001*, and the use of advanced digital compositing, merging computer-generated images together with conventional photographic images, on *Legend of Zu*.

Hong Kong Action Cinema in the Age of Digital Compositing

> I'm concerned about — well, how cyber can we get ... ? Everything is so unreal; one day we find out everything unreal is real ... . We get used to it some years in the future, and we become very doubtful about when something is real. We are indulging in creating something to fool our mind, fool our eyes and fool our senses, to tell you that you are not good enough to judge between real and unreal.
>
> - Tsui Hark, 2000

The production arrangements and narrative forms that shaped the making of Tsui's *Legend of Zu* took place within the development of a new transnational aesthetic based upon the innovative logic of digital compositing.[11] According to the influential critic and cybertheorist Lev Manovich, the contemporary commercial practice of digital compositing needs to be understood in terms of a logic of seamless control over multiple visual elements generated at different times and places, and coordinated in such a way that perception of their real diversity from the audience standpoint is functionally erased.[12] This sort of aesthetic technique tends to be governed by a mutation in cinematic "realism." On the one hand, digital compositors strive for "photorealism," or the seamless integration of diverse visual elements within a framework of visual information identified with standards of photographic precision. On the other hand, digital compositing has taken hold among special effects designers primarily as a way to render realistically images that would either be too difficult or too expensive to model in three-dimensional sculptural form or to photograph outright. That is to say that the digital composite is a profoundly unrealistic, thoroughly illusionistic aesthetic form, which nevertheless strives to match or even outperform basic photographic standards of visual realism.

Fig. 4.1 Digital compositing allows for the seamless construction of photorealistic visual layers

For Manovich, the cultural and political significance of the digital composite lies not only in its often bizarre and contradictory mixtures of realism and illusionism, but in the means by which one produces these new post-photographic images. At the technical level of the means of production he cites a fundamental shift underway between optical and digital technologies, which he identifies with the "resistance to montage" and the rise of a new "aesthetics of continuity." Given the truly massive amounts of digital code involved in producing a single composite shot, designers find it necessary to break up each shot into smaller modules. For instance, a shot from *Jurassic Park* might contain several conventional background elements such as trees and grass, and foreground elements such as human actors and computer-generated dinosaurs. Each one of those elements, including the trees and grass, is either photographed or computer generated independently of the others. The work of cinematography is in many cases transferred over to the work of the compositor who puts together these various pieces through the use of compositing and editing software. Furthermore, each computer-generated element is itself broken down into many smaller components, sometimes called "polygons," which can be manipulated independently of the object as a whole. Thus the cinematic shot becomes extremely malleable all the way down to the basic formal composition of each visual element. The cinema becomes software.

Successful digital compositing erases all traces of origins from its stock of diverse visual elements. Ideally, audiences should never be aware that the shot they are watching did not actually take place, even in a simulated or studio-controlled form. All traces of distinction between layers of visual information should fade before the perception of a single, seamless object. In this sense, the preference of digital designers for an aesthetic of continuity should be clear. With the dramatically increased levels of control over diverse visual elements offered by digital compositing technologies, effects designers could focus in new ways on producing compelling images of continuous change between states of being within a single shot. The rise of the fluid body morph, popularly identified with the work of director James Cameron on *The Abyss* and *Terminator 2*, exemplifies such a concept. No longer would cinematographers need to produce montages of a continuous process staggered by distinct moments of development; they could portray solid objects becoming liquid and then re-solidifying in a single smooth motion. And they could do this with greater levels of precision over time despite the fact that each moment of transition still remained fundamentally a discrete object or visual layer. The camera itself could ultimately be "virtualized" into an extremely mobile perceptual frame, linked in popular terms with the "fly-throughs" of VR displays or the POV controls of recent video games, and identified more with the perspective of the computer screen than with that of any actually-existing camera. With the development of so-called "bullet-time" photography on

The Matrix, cinematic time was fundamentally spatialized, allowing the virtual camera to circle around objects in three-dimensions without moving the narrative forward at all.[13] The movement of the dynamic moving image was given over to dynamics within the shot just as it had formerly been given over to dynamics between shots, without breaking visually with the realist demand for seamless photographic images.

The demand for digitally composited imagery found its greatest world market in the production of action films. This should be unsurprising given the emphasis within action films on audience enjoyment in pure motion, light, and color. Action films have remained among the most significant outlets for digital compositing even as the technology has moved into more subtle areas like the simulation of snow, crowds, hair, lighting, and water, potentially saving time and money for production crews interested in filming those sorts of objects even in more static scenes, without actually having a physical camera present for their recording. Action films, however, took these sorts of practices to extremes, in an escalating arms race toward ever more audacious, and often impossible, martial choreographies. Ultimately, even traditional hallmarks of action filmmaking, such as explosions, fireballs, and stunt doubling could be replicated and controlled as modules of information on a compositor's screen.

It was in this technological context that Hong Kong action cinema made its much-discussed entry into Hollywood during the 1990s. Much of the leap across industries for HK's leading stars and technical talent was made for financial reasons during the post-1997 downturn brought on by the Asian currency crisis and uncertainty over the new role of China in Hong Kong's affairs. In this depressed economic climate, Hong Kong's film producers simply could not meet their financial obligations or keep up with fierce international competition. Financial advantage was not all there was to it though. For a variety of reasons, some aesthetic, some technological, and some financial, the moment of late-1990s was ripe for compositing Hong Kong action cinema together with the effects-driven Hollywood blockbuster.

Generally, the global influence of Hong Kong action cinema among commercial film producers in the US and Europe lay at the choreographic level.[14] Hong Kong action cinema, with Tsui Hark standing among its leading practitioners, cultivated a corporeal vitality that had gone missing in much of Hollywood cinema since the days before the advent of sound reproduction. As David Bordwell puts it, "The Hong Kong tradition challenges filmmakers to come up with ever more inventive ways to display humanity's efforts to burst its earthly bonds."[15] That meant, in the hands of master choreographers like King Hu and Yuen Woo-ping, a seamless display of bodies in motion as they flipped and danced across all visual axes, often in utter violation of terrestrial or gravitational boundaries. It meant refusing to bend images of physical violence and dynamic movement into a strictly realist frame of reference. It meant frequently filming in close-up and in slow motion, displaying an earnest fetish for the visual minutiae of the most improbably moving bodies. All of these traits were applied to the motion of inanimate objects in Hollywood action film. Yet it was only with the rise of digital compositing that designers and audiences voiced a genuine demand for a similar aesthetic of the mobile human body. Hong Kong action cinema provided the requisite imaginary tools and the missing visual links. In exchange, many of Hong Kong's most talented and well-known figures were given the opportunity to work in Hollywood, usually on films like *Mission: Impossible 2* and *The Matrix*, which linked Hong Kong's corporeal choreography to the cutting edges of digital compositing.

The trade-off was not cost-free for either side. While the Hong Kong film industry suffered before the incisors of a high-end talent drain and rampant low-end digital piracy, the core of Hollywood's profit engine was in the midst of a thoroughgoing transformation in visual styles, of a type not seen since the late-1960s when Arthur Penn and Sam Peckinpah unleashed their bloody riffs on the multi-camera cinematography and direction of Akira Kurosawa. Undeniably, Hollywood has gotten the better end of the deal financially, by a staggering order of magnitude, but its victory has come at the cost of an underlying mutation in the national identity of its aesthetics. Hong Kong cinema, at least in the crucial action film genre, now occupies a place at the heart of the dominant global industry as the means of portraying the fluidity of the martial body in motion most commensurate with the fluid visual imagination of the digital age. Of course, one could argue that significant sectors of Hollywood have long voiced a sense of cosmopolitan priorities, based in part on their migrant heritages. Hollywood has long been torn between its standing as the US national film industry, its historical ties to US immigrant populations, and its imperializing impulse to become the national film industry of every nation on earth. Renewal of Hollywood's stagnant image pools has often arrived in the hands of foreign nationals, from the German Expressionists of the 1930s to the European auteurs of the 1960s and 1970s, just as renewal of its bottom lines arrived in the form of global box office receipts during the 1980s and 1990s.[16] The incorporation of Hong Kong action aesthetics has marked a decisive shift in Hollywood's global map, breaking through its long-standing resistance to Asian actors and narratives, realizing to some degree that its global ambitions will be hampered in the short and the long terms if it retains too many fixed attachments to the territory and the nationality of the United States. Its real cosmopolitanism, however, often remains a composite overlay on remarkably centralized cultural industries. The single, seamless object of global Hollywood remains fundamentally fractured just beneath its glossy surface.

The basic paradox is this: while global Hollywood remains predominantly a US affair (excepting Sony's purchase of Columbia

Pictures and Vivendi's purchase of Universal Studios) its markets will increasingly be elsewhere in the world.[17] Hong Kong action cinema, working unevenly in conjunction with the abstract machines of 3-D graphics and digital compositing, has become a key term bridging that potentially fatal divide by enabling Hollywood to resist the appearance of pure-and-simple US exclusivity. Hong Kong's film industry, having been unable to sustain itself in the local market, realized a version of this same problematic some years previously. Evidence of the shift in horizons was found in the 1980s in films like *Zu: Warriors From the Magic Mountain*, even as a round of post-colonial soul-searching engulfed the imaginations of the Hong Kong's young cultural workers. Tsui Hark himself combined the two tendencies perhaps more clearly than anyone else. As a result of their parallel developments, global Hollywood and Hong Kong action cinema have each begun to resemble nodes in an ongoing transnational network of cultural and political sovereignties, where the United States becomes merely one national element, albeit a heavily weighted one, among many. They have become signifiers and symptoms (aesthetically, technologically, and financially) of what Antonio Negri and Michael Hardt have persuasively described as the post-postmodern condition of *Empire*.

Time, Speed and Control: *Legend of Zu* in a Global Frame

The very word "globalization" is a fake. There is no such thing as globalization; there is only virtualization. What is being effectively globalized by instantaneity is time. Everything now happens within the perspective of real time: henceforth we are deemed to live in a "one-time-system."

- Paul Virilio, "Speed and Information"[18]

Michael Hardt and Antonio Negri, among others, have recently argued that the concept and the practice of political sovereignty is undergoing a profound transition, away from its roots in the "imagined communities" of territorial nation-states, towards an emergent transnational order.[19] Whereas the older form of sovereignty, linked not only to the era of the nation-state but to the extension of European sovereignties across the colonial empires, marked off borders and attempted to fix in place flows of power and culture, the new form of sovereignty labeled "Empire" by Hardt and Negri, thrives on perpetual motion and incessant inter-mixtures. The new moment, however, does not mark a passage from geopolitical order to chaos. Instead, they argue, the passage to Empire is from an order of contained differences and exclusive identities to an order of managed differences and hybrid identities. Social order itself, in the form of a deterritorialized political sovereignty, persists and even intensifies, only now in a way that encourages the production of conduits of difference within mobile limits, across widely dispersed territories, where the engagement of power consists primarily in making sure such flows remain more continuous and less erratic over time. In this new condition, inherently global insofar as it is only made possible by the decline of the former Soviet borderlands and the onrush of capital across lines formerly inviolate, social order is threatened from within and without by the possibility of chaotic disturbance, only this time under conditions where appeals to the re-founding of territorial order remain contingent at all points on their outward position within lines of cross-border flow. In this new condition, there is no supra-national source of authority insofar as the mechanisms of order have shifted to the immanent domain of capital, markets and exchange itself. Even the overwhelming power of the US military, arguably the most visibly residual sign of a supra-national imperial order still located in a particular nation-state, is constructed as a sort of transnational "police force" and guarantor of "national security" for the citizens of all advanced capitalist nations. In this new condition, sovereignty itself becomes transposed into the dynamic model of communications and the communications industries, providing a new role for the production of culture and information in the production of an immanent, globally sovereign order.

The production history and the narrative development of *Legend of Zu*, Tsui Hark's problematic addendum to *Zu: Warriors From the Magic Mountain*, offers evidence not only for the visible existence of a new form of deterritorialized global sovereignty, and Hong Kong's distinctive place within it, but also for Tsui Hark's own striking recognition of the changing conditions of global order and his felt need to engage in a revised but not altogether disjunctive set of narratives, representations, and cultural tactics. Neither sequel nor prequel, *Legend of Zu* occupies an autonomous narrative frame that seems both to precede and succeed its "original" at the same time. Whereas *Zu: Warriors From the Magic Mountain* was concerned with the anticipatory construction of fluid cinematic spaces, *Legend of Zu* took those sorts of spaces for granted and centered instead on new questions of time and memory. If the original *Zu* turned in part on imaging ways that China's history and mythology offered visions of technological mastery to rival the greatest Western imperial fantasies, *Legend of Zu* took that vision of futures past even further, into its own uniquely indeterminate temporality. The very idea of setting the more technically advanced version of *Zu* both before and after the original played upon the idea of progress via regress, of a circular or spherical time-space, a non-Euclidean cinematic geometry operating in clear defiance of conventionally modern and Western narratives of linear temporal progress. With cinematic space already being liquefied into a digitally composited miasma, Tsui's imaginary turned toward the liquidation of time and of the identities predicated upon the stability of forward narrative succession. In the process he both echoed and challenged the liquidation of global space into a seamless managerial order dependent increasingly upon control over temporality, speed, and flow. Therein lay both his concept and his critique of the new global order.

Maybe the most remarkable thing about *Legend of Zu* was its insistence on keeping almost every visual element literally afloat for nearly the entire duration of the film. Characters and weapons constantly take flight. Mountains defy gravity. Clouds of blood hang like a shroud over the conflicted land. Amoebic clusters of skulls jab through the painted sky like firebolts, exploding upon impact with the virtuous reprisals of the Kun Lun clan. From the opening credits, which fly upward to the foreground, suspended in brilliantly colored fog as the virtual camera tracks in on them with a series of dizzying zooms, we are thrust into images recalling the closing scenes of *Zu: Warriors*, the fluid space where Ting Yin fights off the merger of the Twin Swords. Sweeping camera movements highlight illusions of three-dimensionality while the visual perspective is deliberately deformed and disoriented by a lack of any fixed point of background focus in the computer-animated atmosphere. The result is a vertiginous, almost free-falling experience, uprooting the audience along with the visual anchors of the cinematic frame.

The narrative begins in the mystical mountainous landscape of Zu, a place of floating boulders and sculpted stone faces, bathed in an ethereal blue-green light. The teacher of the protagonist, King Sky, never identified as the Countess from *Zu: Warriors* but looking almost exactly like a double of Brigitte Lin, laments that she is trapped in this timeless realm, unable to let go of the past. She urges King Sky not to follow her example then transfers her power to him with an assurance that her destiny is in his hands. Just as she does this, a mysterious evil force named Insomnia descends from the distant clouds and blasts through her body. Insomnia dissipates for a moment but the face of King Sky's teacher fragments like eggshells before slowly drifting away. Two hundred years later, King Sky is awakened from a long sleep by the return of the demon Insomnia. The wizard Long Brows, this time called White Brows, tells another warrior, Red, of the systematic targeting of the historic clans. The last holy temple of Omei is next. He must respond quickly by getting all of the humans away from the area at once. On the ground, two warring armies are unaware of the dangers about to confront them. Red and King Sky meet atop a twin peak to plan and mobilize their response.

Fig. 4.2 The digitized face fragments and is revealed as a depthless surface

Although they are called upon to lead the strike against Insomnia, King Sky and Red are temporarily defeated when their own doubles are called upon to fight against them. Insomnia laughs, "[You] can't defeat your own demons." White Brows is called upon to fight against Insomnia with the Sky Mirror, but his weapon is seized from him. Ultimately, the protagonists discover the entire opening sequence of battles has been a trick and a diversion. The true aim of Insomnia is to gain access to the Blood Cave, where it will draw upon the dark energies inside to grow in power until it is immortal and insurmountable. White Brows departs their shared dimension to pursue a more powerful weapon, in replacement for his lost Sky Mirror. He leaves King Sky in charge, and Red to guard the entrance to the Blood Cave. A tiny faerie pays a visit to Red while he watches over the cave, but the faerie turns out to be a demon, which possesses Red and transforms him into an embodiment of Insomnia. Red becomes a brooding king, presiding over the underworld labyrinth of the Blood Cave.

Meanwhile, King Sky has discovered among the warriors of Omei a woman, Enigma, who bears an uncanny resemblance to his teacher of 200 years ago. She is in fact the reincarnation of his teacher, but her memory has been wiped clean. Until she recovers her "true" memory she is unable to fulfill her destiny and play a role in the defeat of Insomnia. The body of Red seems to return to the temple of Omei, but it is a cover for the Phantom Troopers, clad in black leathery armor, who attempt to destroy the remaining temple disciples. These demon warriors clone themselves and move at mind-numbing speeds. They are momentarily defeated by the sudden re-appearance of Enigma. However, when she bends down to check on Red's body she is possessed by the demon inside him and rendered powerless. Red is then unleashed upon the temple, which comes crashing to the ground, but King Sky discovers that he has the ability to fulfill the prophecy of White Brows and unify the forces of Mind, Universe, and Reincarnation. This allows him to rally his forces for a final counter-attack. The blood cloud is unleashed and the world of humans is rendered a wasteland. King Sky descends into the underworld to confront the possessed Red and find the body of Enigma. She is restored to life as her spirit is rescued from the mind of Red. As a final battle between King Sky and Red ensues she launches skyward to unify the Twin Swords, accelerate to the "speed of light" and defeat the Blood Demon that has emerged from the Blood Cloud. In the process, her memory of her immortal self returns and she is both healed and destroyed at once in a massive inferno. Yet, the possibility that she might one day be re-created remains. The temple is reconstructed and a new generation inaugurated, as King Sky departs at top speed into the clouds.

Among the more remarkable features of *Legend of Zu*, despite its apparent concern for the fate of the human armies, is its almost complete disinterest in the terrestrial realms. The film's early battle above the armies about to be evacuated is one of the only times that *Legend of Zu* ever descends from the ethereal. And even then, the battle is elaborately airborne and supernatural. This stands in stark contrast to *Zu: Warriors From the Magic Mountain*, which concerned itself primarily with the dynamics between the terrestrial and the ethereal. *Legend of Zu* largely leaves behind that dynamic, in favor of the frictionless conflicts among the immortals themselves. It is almost as if the conflicts among humans have been erased, if not actually resolved, insofar as the film no longer considers them of any real narrative significance. The armies are there merely to be evacuated. When the general voices his initial opposition in the blustery tones of militaristic bravado he is almost immediately shown to be unaware of his real peril. The real action lies in the high-speed realm above and below the ground.

The forces of evil, dominance and singularity that had been contained throughout most of *Zu: Warriors* (i.e. – the Blood Demon) are in *Legend of Zu* running amok. Technologies of the visual have advanced, in narrative step with an increasing focus on the super-heroic characters, and yet evil is rampaging uncontained across the lands, imagined this time as a nightmarish, high-speed cluster of skulls. Times, we might say, have changed. As the opening voice-over states, "Always a mountain higher, a horizon more. The universe in its vastness is forever changing." And yet, these times are occurring both before and after *Zu: Warriors*, returning us at once to a deeper mythical past that seems to stretch out ahead and behind in a limitless train. These are the conflicts that will shape the fortunes of the characters in *Zu: Warriors*, apparently in direct linear descent, yet King Sky and Red nevertheless describe them as the eternal pull of forces between yang and yin, cycling forever across the mythically spatialized timescape.

The eternal fails to cancel or erase the linear, even as it detaches from the terrestrial. As much as the film signifies itself inside narratives of moral struggle between good and evil, it signifies itself also within a play between linear and circular time frames. It is in that exact sense that we can understand the desires of King Sky's teacher to exit the stifling realm of limitless time (as she remarks at the start, "Two hundred years, how time flies!"), only later to be reborn and die simultaneously. The plot hurtles us forward, to the point of rebirth, which is also imagined circularly as the point of death, the recovery and the erasure of memory and subjectivity. Following Paul Virilio, we might say the narrative approaches an image of "limit speed," in which all temporal moments coincide.[20]

Having virtualized space and liquidated time into the narrative problematics of immortality and reincarnation, experienced by the characters both as a form of salvation and as the trauma of a world without exit, *Legend of Zu* articulates the fundamental ambivalences of its historical moment. Although generally lacking in the humorous self-awareness and stark modernist coloration of its predecessor, *Legend of Zu* is not lacking in serious reflections on its times. Its reflections, however, seem further removed this time into allegory, with the narrative paced at such a frantic speed that one practically has to slow the film down to still frames to perceive its thickets of meaning and its grappling with the cultural and political problematics of Empire.

The turn to the problem of time and memory under conditions of high-speed virtualization signifies a deep dissatisfaction with a world in which time itself has seemed to stand still, where the speed of the present resolves the past and the future into a perpetual blur, where every time becomes the same time. The struggle engaged in by the characters in *Legend of Zu* is to find a way out of this perpetual moment, and thus to defeat the powers of singularity and domination. Thus it is not true for them that the present contains too little time, in the obviously frantic speed-up of globalized capitalism, but *too much*. If post-national sovereignty evaporates into what Negri and Hardt call the "non-place of Empire," then it is surely in the surplus of time, or more precisely, in the multiple, proliferating times and speeds of the cross-border flows and slipstreams that define the new global order, that the crisis of the present may ultimately be discovered. This cultural problematic resonates strongly with the technical problematic of digital compositing, with its intensified control over the time-space of the image. Therein lies the allegorical value of Tsui's *Legend of Zu*. Through its lens, we have all become like King Sky's melancholy teacher, brooding over the conditions of our own surplus, desperate for a path back into the time of decay and crisis, the time of humanity as imperfection and limit. The very extensibility of Empire, a form of power spanning across all spaces and times because it operates immanently to the society itself, thus appearing as an integral system without exterior, is the contemporary nightmare from which we struggle to awaken.

Unfortunately, neither its dense allegorical discourse, nor its frames chock full of digital eye candy, could save *Legend of Zu* from the commercial fate of *Zu: Warriors From the Magic Mountain*. Despite being released in the wake of the worldwide *wuxia* craze that trailed the success of *Crouching Tiger, Hidden Dragon*, despite a distribution contract signed as a co-production agreement with the powerful US mini-studio Miramax, and despite a miniscule budget (for an effects-driven action film) of HK$90 million helped in part by a daring bout of unauthorized shooting in mainland China, *Legend of Zu* bombed at the box office practically everywhere. In a remarkably little-noticed act of overt censorship, the film was withdrawn from the twenty-sixth annual Hong Kong International Film Festival because of a policy decision handed down from Beijing, designed to punish unauthorized filming on the mainland. Yet its failings had little to do with state censorship.

Once again, Tsui seemed to be running too fast and too far ahead of his audience. With the shadow of *Star Wars* (this time the practically all-digital critical flop, *Episode I*) looming over his work once again, many critics complained that *Legend of Zu* was no longer even a martial arts film. It was something else, not yet fully classifiable. Few could make up their minds about whether or not they liked it. The action had been transposed entirely into the magical and the virtual. Many complained, above and beyond the advanced compression technology of the film's difficult-to-follow plot line, that it was often little more than a single continuous effects shot. Tsui himself came in for the sort of criticism that he alternately directed at Lucas, with many arguing that he had become too enamored of the apparent limitlessness of the virtual to pay much attention anymore to the earthly concerns of his characters. A sort of nausea set in as audiences labored to keep up with the flow of the plot at the same time that the camera refused to come to rest from its dazzling vertiginous leaps. Whether those same audiences will some day remember *Legend of Zu* as the same sort of anticipatory leap beyond the present that they were not yet prepared to make, as some once did with its predecessor, is something that yet remains to be seen.

5

Conclusion
The Meanings of *Zu*

In the wake of the extraordinary worldwide success of Ang Lee's *wuxia* epic, *Crouching Tiger, Hidden Dragon*, critics and representatives of the Hong Kong Film industry felt equally justified in heaving a collective sigh of relief. Who could blame them? After all, the industry had just been through one of the worst downturns in its history following the currency crisis and the Chinese handover in 1997. Surely, an international hit on the magnitude of *Crouching Tiger* was just what it needed to make the case for its continuing creative and commercial vitality. It was not too long before studio executives began to crow about the ways that *Crouching Tiger* marked the beginning of a new era in Hong Kong cinema, defined by increasing exports of Chinese culture, integration of pan-Chinese ethnicities, and the final adoption of Hollywood's disciplined and rationalized mode of production by Hong Kong's notoriously anarchic production houses. There is no question that the local box office has recovered from its low point of five years past. Yet, the failure to follow up on the success of *Crouching Tiger* in any notable way, up to and including the inability of Tsui Hark to generate much audience interest outside Hong Kong itself in *Legend of Zu*, poses a continuing dilemma for the industry as a whole.

Arguably, much of the late-1990s wave of excitement over Hong Kong action cinema has also died down substantially. Of course there will be a prequel to *Crouching Tiger*. John Woo will remain near the A-list of Hollywood directors despite the *Windtalkers* fiasco. Jackie Chan remains an institution whose recent mastery of the biracial buddy picture caps an illustrious career. Th*e Matrix* sequels will keep Yuen Woo-ping in the limelight for all of 2003, and likely for some time to come. Yet, there is a palpable sense right now that much of the recent wave of Hong Kong's influence over the global imaginary has been more-or-less absorbed into the day-to-day mechanics of Hollywood.

Hong Kong is not elsewhere anymore it is everywhere, blasted throughout the circuitry of the global mediasphere. Martial arts aesthetics in mainstream commercial cinema are becoming more and more the products of simulation than of the years of physical training, undergone by people such as Yuen Biao and Sammo Hung, making them even more accessible to choreographers and film directors from outside Hong Kong. Tsui Hark has contributed as much as anyone, for better or worse, to the current state of affairs, yet despite the critical accolades bestowed on *Time and Tide*, he remains primarily a niche phenomenon. Often, he functions more as the poster child for the crisis itself, a sort of spectre of cultural mistranslation and global disjunction. To many aficionados, this remains one of the central ongoing mysteries of the past two decades in Hong Kong cinema.

To some degree, Tsui's long-term standing as a doubled symbol of creation and crisis in Hong Kong cinema really began with *Zu: Warriors From the Magic Mountain*, and came full circle with *Legend of Zu*. Indeed, considering its pedigree no one should be too surprised that *Legend of Zu* failed to catch the tailwinds of

Crouching Tiger, Hidden Dragon and *The Matrix*. Hand wringing over profits and loss is the easy part though. The more difficult task consists of returning to *Zu: Warriors From the Magic Mountain* with an eye on the basic shifts in the cultural and cinematic imaginary of Hong Kong that it was trying to effect, as a way of returning to the present with viable categories for understanding the possible aftermath of the current crisis. In that context it is important to recall that Tsui's strategy on *Zu: Warriors* was far from conservative. *Zu: Warriors* aimed to make connections which others were either unwilling to try or unable to see. It is in that sense of its constructive connections that we can now retrospectively call *Zu: Warriors* an "anticipatory" work of popular culture. It articulated networks and pathways, pried open genres, gambled on strategies, forced untried collisions, and mixed explosive compounds. The fact that not all of them worked out immediately should deter no one from considering their ultimate dimensions. For, from its crisis, at least in part, emerged both the golden age of Hong Kong cinema and the emergent problems of global cultural, technological, and financial integration as the future horizons of Hong Kong cinema.

In the end, how should we best understand the long-term outcome of *Zu: Warriors From the Magic Mountain*? There are at least two general routes, although these two contain multitudes, some parts intended, others not. We might describe all of them as variations on hostility to binary patterns of imagination. On the one hand, it made the leap into direct contestation with mainstream Hollywood without sacrificing either its political and intellectual savvy or its local and regional roots. This means that it refused the binary opposition between Hollywood and Hong Kong, or more abstractly, between the global and the local. To a certain extent, this type of refusal was already a hallmark of the postmodern Hong Kong cinema, which set the stage for *Zu: Warriors* by establishing as normal industrial routine the practices of both citational and non-citational cross-cultural "borrowing." However, *Zu: Warriors* took it a major step further by building in a self-reflexive discourse on its own conventions and elevating the narrative into an allegorical articulation of Hong Kong's post-colonial predicament by clearing space between globality and nationality for social autonomy. One needn't evacuate the local in order to participate in the global. It was more than a little bit appropriate then, given Tsui's hostility toward binary oppositions of all kinds, that the form of such a complex social allegory took shape at the intersection of deceptively simple genres like Wuxia and the pseudo-Hollywood special effects blockbuster. It is also in that anti-binary context that Tsui's repeated gender subversions make their most sense as much larger allegorical figures.

On the other hand, in a related fashion, *Zu: Warriors* effectively refuted the idea that traditional martial arts choreography could not coexist with the sorts of optical illusions being pumped out by Hollywood's newly invigorated special effects teams. In fact, it proved quite the opposite. By merging the capacities of optical effects technologies to represent fluid changes in state over time with the capacities of martial arts choreography to represent fluid bodily motion across three dimensions within the cinematic frame, *Zu: Warriors* produced a new type of dynamic and fluid cinematic space. To an increasing degree over the next two decades, that type of cinematic space gained ground as the dominant visual imagination of the emergent digital effects technologies, paving the way eventually, for better or worse, for the technical and stylistic merger between Hong Kong and Hollywood action cinemas in the mid-1990s. At the same time, Tsui insisted on developing his own local effects production house, allowing him to continue working in the future outside of a relation of dependency on US-based design houses, a tendency which has proved anticipatory in the age of runaway effects production, from the US toward the other side of the Pacific Rim, in the first years of the twenty-first century. Once again, desire for an autonomous locality returns from within the heart of global culture, without necessarily sacrificing its place in the network of global relations.

The pattern of opposition to simple oppositions continued in *Legend of Zu*, although the preoccupation with space was transferred to a concern with time. Concerns over a singular, timeless existence, one that denied desire to the subject insofar as it negated the possibility of transformation, limitation, and death, played out across a hyperkinetic succession of digital composites. Fluid change of states, erasing perceptions of actually diverse origins, enabled by digital visual technologies, became a cry for the friction and heft of history amid the weightlessness of a virtual culture. Yet the only way Tsui seems to know how to work is from the inside out, in this case producing a version of the weightless virtual even as he registers its dangers and frustrations. In that sense, the final evasion might be of the traditional dictates of politicized aesthetics. Rather than producing an actual counter-discourse, Tsui revels in the play of negation, ambivalence, and ambiguity itself. The new transnational culture and politics, which forms the background to *Legend of Zu*'s production and its narrative, is not something to oppose or to support, but simply a new context for action. Tsui Hark is simply relaying to us ways that that context might be made more socially navigable. The outcome of his labors ought to be measured in the capillary streams branching off from his images and his practices, in the future mutations derived afterward, not necessarily in the internal virtues of the works themselves. And in that exact sense, the twenty-year old-question of *Zu*'s success or failure, measured strictly in terms of the financial health and well-being of the Hong Kong film industry, is finally beside the point.

Notes

Chapter 1   Seeing Past the Future

1   Lisa Morton, *The Cinema of Tsui Hark* (Jefferson, NC and London: McFarland & Company, Inc. Publishers, 2001), p. 50.
2   David Bordwell, Planet Hong Kong (Cambridge, MA: Harvard University Press, 2000), p. 136.
3   This basic narrative is framed well by recent publications and exhibitions at the Hong Kong Film Archive. See, for instance, Law Kar and Winnie Fu, eds., *Hong Kong Cinema: From Handicraft to High Tech* (Hong Kong: Hong Kong Film Archive, 2000). On Tsui Hark more specifically, see Sam Ho, ed., *The Swordsman and His Jiang Hu: Tsui Hark and Hong Kong Film* (Hong Kong: Hong Kong Film Archive, 2001).

Chapter 2   Speeding Towards Autonomy

1   Ackbar Abbas, *Hong Kong: Culture and the Politics of Disappearance* (Minneapolis, MN: University of Minnesota Press, 1997), p. 4.

2   On the debate over post-colonial narrative and the question of "national allegory" see Frederic Jameson, "Third World Literature in the Era of Multinational Capital," *Social Text*, Fall 1986, pp. 65–88, and the response by Aijaz Ahmad, "Jameson's Rhetoric of Otherness and the 'National Allegory'," in *In Theory: Classes, Nations, Literatures* (New York: Verso, 1992), pp. 95–122.

3   Observations of Tsui's so-called nationalism range from the classic work of Steven Teo in *Hong Kong Cinema: The Extra Dimensions* (London: BFI Press, 1997), to Lisa Stokes and Michael Hoover, *City on Fire* (New York: Verso, 1998), to an intriguing recent article by Cindy Chan Shu-ching, "Colonial Modernity: A Study of Tsui Hark's Production and Films," *E-Journal of Hong Kong Cultural and Social Studies*, March 2002, http://www.hku.hk/hkcsp/ccex/ehkcss01, where she argues that Tsui Hark's working methods are defined by community bonds echoing a model of the Confucian family.

4   Abbas, *Hong Kong*, pp. 10–15.

5   On the politics of the Hong Kong New Wave see the essays by Law and Hector Rodriguez in Esther Yau, ed., *At Full Speed: Hong Kong Cinema in a Borderless World* (Minneapolis, MN: University of Minnesota Press, 2001).

6   On the history of Hong Kong's post-colonial transition see Jan Morris, *Hong Kong: Epilogue to an Empire*. Revised ed. (New York: Vintage Books, 1997) and Steven Tsang, *Hong Kong: An Appointment with China* (London and New York: I. B. Tauris, 1997).

7   Saskia Sassen, *The Global City: New York, London, Tokyo* (Princeton, NJ: Princeton University Press, 2001); Anthony King, *Urbanism, Colonialism and the World Economy: Cultural and Spatial Foundations of the World Urban System* (London and New York: Routledge, 1990).

8   Teo himself has led the way towards such a re-formulation, as we can see in the differences between his interpretation of Tsui Hark's "nationalism" in *Hong Kong Cinema: The Extra Dimensions* (London: BFI Press, 1997) and his more recent article, "Tsui Hark: National Style and Polemic" from Esther Yau, ed., *At Full Speed: Hong Kong Cinema in a Borderless World* (Minneapolis, MN: University of Minnesota Press, 1999). In the earlier version he understands Tsui

Hark's worldview in rather strictly nationalism terms. "Tsui depicts the mythic world of the martial arts as a time when China's sciences and inventions were at their peak. This notion of Chinese science and military prowess, combined with popular mythologising of the martial arts, form the substance of Tsui's nationalist theme." (p. 163) However, in the later essay, Teo argues that Tsui's "notion of speed overrides the theme of nationalism" (p. 147).

9   On Bruce Lee and cultural modernity see Jachinson Chan, *Chinese American Masculinities: From Fu Manchu to Bruce Lee* (New York: Routledge, 2001), Tony Rayns, "Bruce Lee: Narcissism and Nationalism" from *A Study of the Hong Kong Martial Arts Film* (Hong Kong International Film Festival Publications) pp. 109–12, and Steven Teo, "Narcissus and the Little Dragon," in *Hong Kong Cinema: The Extra Dimensions.*

10   Lisa Morton, *The Cinema of Tsui Hark*, p. 13.

11   Edward Said, *Orientalism* (New York: Pantheon, 1977), p. 7.

12   On Spivak and the concept of "erasure" see her introduction to Jacques Derrida, *Of Grammatology* (Baltimore, MD: Johns Hopkins University Press, 1976).

13   David Bordwell, *Planet Hong Kong*, p. 12.

14   Akbar Abbas, *Hong Kong*, pp. 12–14.

Chapter 3   Uneven Developments

1   Frederic Jameson, "Culture and Finance Capital," in *The Cultural Turn* (New York: Verso, 1998), pp. 136–161.

2   Evans Chan, "Postmodernism and Hong Kong Cinema," in Arif Dirlik and Xudong Zhang, eds., *Postmodernism and China* (Durham, NC: Duke University Press, 2000), pp. 294–322.

3   "In this passage to a space whose curvature is no longer that of the real, nor of truth, the age of simulation thus begins with a liquidation of all referentials — worse: by their artificial resurrection in systems of signs, which are a more ductile material than meaning, in that they lend themselves to all systems of equivalence, all binary oppositions and all combinatory algebra. It is no longer a question of imitation,

nor of reduplication, nor even of parody. It is rather a question of substituting signs of the real for the real itself; that is, an operation to deter every real process by its operational double, a metastable, programmatic, perfect descriptive machine which provides all the signs of the real and short-circuits all its vicissitudes. Never again will the real have to be produced: this is the vital function of the model in a system of death, or rather of anticipated resurrection which no longer leaves any chance even in the event of death. A hyperreal henceforth sheltered from the imaginary, and from any distinction between the real and the imaginary, leaving room only for the orbital recurrence of models and the simulated generation of difference." Jean Baudrillard, *Simulacra and Simulations,* in Mark Poster, ed., *Jean Baudrillard: Selected Writings* (Palo Alto, CA: Stanford University Press, 1988) pp. 166–184.

4   Jameson, "Culture and Finance Capital."

5   On the phantasmagoria, cinema and special effects, see Lev Manovich, *The Language of New Media* (Cambridge, MA: MIT Press, 2000), p. 296. Also see Walter Benjamin's writings on the Parisian arcades of the nineteenth century as immersive phantasmagoria in his *The Arcades Project,* (Cambridge, MA: Harvard University Press, 2000).

6   There is an excellent passage in Antonio Negri and Michael Hardt's *Empire* that makes the case for a "phantasmagoric" image of global cultural and capital flow quite persuasively by linking it with Guy Debord's theory of "spectacle." In their chapter on the "Mixed Constitution" of Empire they write, "In effect, the glue that holds together the diverse functions and bodies of the hybrid constitution is what Guy Debord called the spectacle, an integrated and diffuse apparatus of images and ideas that produces and regulates public discourse and opinion. In the society of the spectacle, what was once imagined as the public sphere, the open terrain of political exchange and participation, completely evaporates. The spectacle destroys any collective form of sociality – individualizing social actors in their separate automobiles and in front of separate video screens – and at the same time imposes a new mass sociality, a new uniformity of action and thought. On this spectacular terrain, tradition forms of struggle

over the constitution become inconceivable." Negri and Hardt, *Empire* (Cambridge, MA: Harvard University Press, 2000).

7   See Homi K. Bhabha, "Of Mimicry and Man: The Ambivalence of Colonial Discourse," in *The Location of Culture* (New York: Routledge, 1994).

8   On theories of "proto-simulation" and immersion see Marie-Laure Ryan, "Immersion v. Interactivity: Virtual Reality and Literary Theory," *Postmodern Culture*, vol. 5, no. 1, September, 1994, and Scott Bukatman, "Terminal Penetration," in *Terminal Identity: The Virtual Subject in Postmodern Science Fiction* (Durham, NC: Duke University Press, 1993).

9   On the New Hollywood and blockbuster economics see Janet Wasko, Hollywood in the Information Age, (Austin, TX: University of Texas Press, 1994) and "Adjusting to the New Global Economy: Hollywood in the 1990s," in Albert Moran, ed., *Film Policy: International, National and Regional Perspectives* (New York: Routledge, 1996).

10 The "bubble economy" is normally defined as a macro-economic condition in which asset prices, such as stocks and real estate, rise at a rate much higher than might be predicted based upon "economic fundamentals" such as productivity and output. This sort of condition is commonly associated with a frenzied pace of speculative buying, or purchases of stocks and real estate on the basis of unrealized future value rather than existing present value. Hong Kong's rise as a financial capital, along with the Japan's economy in the 1980s and the US tech economy in the 1990s are all good examples of "bubble economies."

11 See <http://www.hkmdb.com/hk/awards/hkfa_nom-83.html>.

12 There are some sporadic signs that *Zu: Warriors From the Magic Mountain* played a role in the visual imaginations of certain Hollywood directors and art designers during the 1980s. Sam Raimi, director of the *Evil Dead* series and recently of *Spiderman*, cited *Zu: Warriors* during interviews in the 1980s as one of his inspirations for the cheap but effective visual effects on *Evil Dead*. Even more directly, John Carpenter cited it as the film most responsible for his visual design on *Big Trouble in Little China*.

13 Tsui himself both acknowledges and downplays their influence in current interviews. "We also had some people out from L.A., who had

done *Star Wars*, and they gave us a lot of information and knowledge about the way we handled some of the shots." Quoted from Lisa Morton, *The Cinema of Tsui Hark* (Jefferson, NC: McFarland & Co., Inc., 2001), p. 53. In this quote Tsui makes clear that these workers played merely an advisory role, while flattening their individual contributions and muting some of their connections to the leading technical tendencies of the moment.

14   Tsui Hark quoted from Lisa Morton, *The Cinema of Tsui Hark*, p. 53.

15   Max Fleischer's second series, *Out of the Inkwell* (1919) was the first to combine hand-drawn animation and photographic images. On Fleischer and the rotoscope see Richard Rickitt, *Special Effects: The History and Technique* (New York: Billboard Books, 2000).

16   Michelle Pierson, *Special Effects: Still in Search of Wonder* (New York: Columbia University Press, 2002).

17   Michel De Certeau, *The Practice of Everyday Life*, fourth edition (Berkeley, CA: University of California Press, 2002), p. 117.

18   Henri Lefebvre, *The Production of Space* (London: Blackwell, 1991).

19   On Melies see Elizabeth Ezra, *Georges Melies: The Birth of the Auteur* (Manchester, UK: Manchester University Press, 2000).

20   On Virilio and the concept of "real time" see "The Perspective of Real Time" in Paul Virilio, *Open Sky* (New York: Verso, 1997).

Chapter 4   Technologies of Transnationalism

1   Michael Hardt and Antonio Negri, *Empire* (Cambridge, MA: Harvard University Press, 2000), p. 346.

2   Among the few sites available on the Web distributing information about *Zu: Time Warriors* is the following: <http://www.brns.com/pages4/7fort57.html>.

3   Cinema City was founded in 1980 by Karl Maka, Dean Shek and Raymond Wong. Their primary interest as independent producers was to make a series of madcap comedies in the tradition of Michael Hui. Their greatest commercial success was the *Aces Go Places* series, which put them into close contact with Tsui Hark. After the founding of Film

Workshop, the two companies worked together on many of Film Workshop's seminal early films, such as *Shanghai Blues*.

4   On the concept of "auteurism" and its material role both in Hollywood and in other world cinemas see Timothy Corrigan, "Auteurs in the New Hollywood," in Jon Lewis, ed., *The New American Cinema* (Durham, NC: Duke University Press, 1998).

5   <http://www.filmworkshop.net>.

6   On the history of Industrial Light and Magic see Mark Cotta Vaz and Patricia Rose Duignan, *Industrial Light and Magic: Into the Digital Realm* (New York: Ballantine, 1996).

7   See "The New International Division of Hollywood Labor," in Toby Miller, ed., *Global Hollywood* (Berkeley, CA: University of California Press, 2001).

8   *Logik: For the Digitally Correct* (Discreet Logic, Inc. Newsletter), Issue no. 3, 1995.

9   See *Hong Kong Cinema: From Handicraft to High Tech* (Hong Kong Film Archive, 2001).

10   On personalism and Tsui Hark's working methods see Cindy Chan Shu-ching, "Colonial Modernity: A Study of Tsui Hark's Production and Films," *E-Journal of Hong Kong Cultural and Social Studies*, March 2002,< http://www.hku.hk/hkcsp/ccex/ehkcss01>.

11   This section is based upon work presented at the Center for Asian Studies in December of 2001, and published in the *E-Journal of Hong Kong Cultural and Social Studies*, Issue 1, February 2002. <http://www.hku.hk/hkcsp/ccex/ehkcss01/a_pdf12.htm>.

12   Lev Manovich, *The Language of New Media* (Cambridge, MA: MIT Press, 2001) pp. 136–60.

13   On "bullet-time" and special effects in *The Matrix* see Kevin H. Martin, "Jacking Into The Matrix," *Cinefex*, no. 79, May 1999.

14   There are a couple of scenes early in Olivier Assayas's film *Irma Vep* where the French crew coordinating Maggie Cheung's performance, including a director clearly intended as a play on Luc Besson, rhapsodize about the ballistic beauty of John Woo. These scenes pretty much encapsulate this idea.

15   Bordwell, *Planet Hong Kong*, p. 220.

16   On the historical cosmopolitanism of Hollywood see Saverio

Giovacchini, *Hollywood Modernism* (Philadelphia, PA: Temple University Press, 2001).

17   See Toby Miller, ed., *Global Hollywood* (Berkeley, CA: University of California Press, 2001).

18   Paul Virilio, "Speed and Information: Cyberspace Alarm!", *Ctheory.net*, August, 1995.

19   See Negri and Hardt, *Empire*, Part 2.

20   On time, globalism and virtuality, see Paul Virilio, "Continental Drift," in *Open Sky* (New York: Verso 1997).

Filmography

**Zu: Warriors From the Magic Mountain /
Shushan: Xin Shushan jianxia (蜀山：新蜀山劍俠)**

Hong Kong 1983

Director
Tsui Hark

Producer
Leonard Ho

Screenplay
Shui Chung-yuet
Roy Szeto Cheuk-hon
Jerrold Mundis

Director of Photography
Christopher Doyle

Cinematographers
Bill Wong
Raymond Lam

Action Choreographers
Corey Yuen Kwai
Yuen Biao
Fung Hak-on
Mang Hoi

Editor
Peter Cheung

Art Directors
Oliver Wong
William Chang

Music
Kwan Sing-yau

Production Company
Golden Harvest Productions

Executive Producer
Raymond Chow

Assistant Producer
Leonard Ho

Production Manager
Chow Chi-man

Assistant Directors
Yeung Wah
Lam Tze-wan

Costumes
Chu Sing-hei

Special Effects

Robert Blalack

Peter Kuran

Arnie Wong

John Scheele

Tama Takahashi

Cast

Yuen Biao (元彪)	as Ti Ming-chi (狄明奇)
Sammo Hung (洪金寶)	as Long Brows (長眉真人)
Adam Cheng Siu-chow (鄭少秋)	as Ting Yin (丁引)
Damian Lau Chung-yun (劉松仁)	as Abbott Hsiao Yu (曉如禪師)
Mang Hoi (孟海)	as Yi Chen (一真)
Brigitte Lin (林青霞)	as The Countess (瑤池堡主)
Moon Lee Choi-fung (李賽鳳)	as Countess's Guard (瑤池侍衛/若蘭)
Hsia Guang-li (夏光莉)	as Chi Wu-shuang (姬無霜)
Tsui Siu-keung (徐少強)	as Heaven's Blade (天刀)
Judy Ong (翁倩玉)	as Li I-chi (李亦奇)
Dick Wei (狄威)	as First Commander (左統領)
Chung Fat (鍾發)	as Second Commander (右統領)
Tsui Hark (徐克)	as Zu Soldier (蜀山侍衛)

Distributor

Golden Harvest Productions

Duration

92.5 minutes

Format

1: 1.85

Camera

Panavision

97 minutes 3 seconds

Dolby

In Colour Subtitles

Selected Bibliography

A few of the following books and essays deal with Zu: Warriors From the Magic Mountain *directly; others, directly or indirectly, give it context.*

Abbas, Ackbar. 1997. *Hong Kong: Culture and the Politics of Disappearance.* Minneapolis, MN: University of Minnesota Press.

Ahmad, Aijaz. 1992. "Jameson's Rhetoric of Otherness and the 'National Allegory'" in *In Theory: Classes, Nations, Literatures.* New York: Verso.

Balio, Tino. 1996. "Adjusting to the New Global Economy: Hollywood in the 1990s" in Moran, Albert, ed. *Film Policy: International, National and Regional Perspectives.* New York: Routledge.

Baudrillard, Jean. 1988. "Simulacra and Simulations" in Poster, Mark, ed. *Jean Baudrillard: Selected Writings.* Palo Alto, CA: Stanford University Press.

Benjamin, Walter. 2000. *The Arcades Project.* Cambridge, MA: Harvard University Press.

Bhabha, Homi K. 1994. "Of Mimicry and Man: The Ambivalence of Colonial Discourse" in *The Location of Culture.* New York: Routledge.

Bordwell, David. 2000. *Planet Hong Kong*. Cambridge, MA: Harvard University Press.

Bukatman, Scott, ed. 1993. "Terminal Penetration" in *Terminal Identity: The Virtual Subject in Postmodern Science Fiction*. Durham, NC: Duke University Press.

Chan, Evans. 2000. "Postmodernism and Hong Kong Cinema" in Dirlik, Arif and Zhang, Xudong, eds. 2000. *Postmodernism and China*. Durham, NC: Duke University Press.

Chan, Jachinson. 2001. *Chinese American Masculinities: From Fu Manchu to Bruce Lee*. New York: Routledge.

Chan Shu-ching, Cindy. 2002 "Colonial Modernity: A Study of Tsui Hark's Production and Films." *E-Journal of Hong Kong Cultural and Social Studies*. (March).

Cotta Vaz, Mark and Rose Duignan, Patricia. 1996. *Industrial Light and Magic: Into the Digital Realm*. New York: Ballantine.

De Certeau, Michel. 2002. *The Practice of Everyday Life*. Fourth edition. Berkeley, CA: University of California Press.

Ezra, Elizabeth. 2000. *Georges Melies: The Birth of the Auteur*. Manchester, UK: Manchester University Press.

Giovacchini, Saverio. 2001. *Hollywood Modernism*. Philadelphia, PA: Temple University Press.

Hardt, Michael and Negri, Antonio. 2000. *Empire*. Cambridge, MA: Harvard University Press.

Ho, Sam, ed. 2001. *The Swordsman and His Jiang Hu: Tsui Hark and Hong Kong Film*. Hong Kong: Hong Kong Film Archive.

Jameson, Frederic. 1998. "Culture and Finance Capital" in *The Cultural Turn*. New York: Verso.

———. 1986. "Third World Literature in the Era of Multinational Capital," *Social Text* (Fall).

Kar, Law and Fu, Winnie, eds. 2000. *Hong Kong Cinema: From Handicraft to High Tech*. Hong Kong: Hong Kong Film Archive.

King, Anthony. 1990. *Urbanism, Colonialism and the World Economy: Cultural and Spatial Foundations of the World Urban System*. London and New York: Routledge.

Lefebvre, Henri. 1991 *The Production of Space*. London: Blackwell.

Lewis, Jon, ed. 1998. *The New American Cinema*. Durham, NC: Duke University Press.

Manovich, Lev. 2001. *The Language of New Media*. Cambridge, MA: MIT Press.

Martin, Kevin H. 1999. "Jacking Into The Matrix." *Cinefex*, no. 79. (May).

Miller, Toby, ed. 2001. *Global Hollywood*. Berkeley, CA: University of California Press.

Morris, Jan. 1997. *Hong Kong: Epilogue to an Empire*. Revised ed. New York: Vintage Books.

Morton, Lisa. 2001. *The Cinema of Tsui Hark*. Jefferson, NC and London: McFarland & Company, Inc.

Pierson, Michelle. 2002. *Special Effects: Still in Search of Wonder*. New York: Columbia University Press.

Rickitt, Richard. 2000. *Special Effects: The History and Technique*. New York: Billboard Books.

Ryan, Marie-Laure. 1994. "Immersion v. Interactivity: Virtual Reality and Literary Theory." *Postmodern Culture*, vol. 5, no. 1 (September).

Said, Edward. 1977. *Orientalism*. New York: Pantheon.

Sassen, Saskia. 2001. *The Global City: New York, London, Tokyo*. Princeton, NJ: Princeton University Press.

Spivak, Gayatri. 1976. "Introduction" in Derrida, Jacques. 1976. *Of Grammatology*. Baltimore, MD: Johns Hopkins University Press.

Stokes, Lisa and Hoover, Michael. 1998. *City on Fire*. New York: Verso.

Teo, Steven. 1997. *Hong Kong Cinema: The Extra Dimensions*. London: BFI Press.

Tsang, Steven. 1997. *Hong Kong: An Appointment With China*. London and New York: I. B. Tauris.

Virilio, Paul. 1997. *Open Sky*. New York: Verso.

——. 1995. "Speed and Information: Cyberspace Alarm!" *Ctheory.net* (August).

Wasko, Janet. 1994. *Hollywood in the Information Age*. Austin, TX: University of Texas Press.

Yau, Esther, ed. 2001. *At Full Speed: Hong Kong Cinema in a Borderless World*. Minneapolis, MN: University of Minnesota Press.